THE **POWER** OF **MOVING** **FORWARD**

SEEING ALCHEMY IN LIFE

OVERCOMING PRESENT-DAY CHALLENGES USING ANCIENT WISDOM

CARLA MORRIS WEIS, MD

Mother, Physician and Metaphysician

Healer, Teacher, and Guide in the Great Mystery School

Lineage of King Salomon (The Modern Mystery School)

authorHOUSE®

AuthorHouse™
1663 Liberty Drive
Bloomington, IN 47403
www.authorhouse.com
Phone: 833-262-8899

Published by AuthorHouse   07/12/2023

ISBN: 979-8-8230-0919-5 (sc)
ISBN: 979-8-8230-0918-8 (e)

Library of Congress Control Number: 2023909853

Original Symbol Design
Page 200
Gudni Gudnason

Book Cover Design
MCD Advertising
David Davis
310-251-6926
david@mc-adv.com

Illustrations Credit
Lucy Lazure
916-224-7277
www.lucylazure.com
lucy@lucylazure.com

Print information available on the last page.

Dedication

This book is dedicated to my mother and father. They have loved me deeply and no matter what. They have played their part so that I could play mine, and I am eternally grateful.

To my five beautiful daughters: I love you more than I ever believed a human could love. You have each taught me so very much and have expanded my ability to experience joy in this world. It is because of the great beauty you each hold within you that I have been able to see my own. You have saved my life more than once. Thank you. You are all my favorite.

To my three brothers: Thank you for being stellar examples of men in this world. I am honored and proud to call you my brothers, and I love you.

To my grandparents, and all my ancestors: Your DNA and your spirit runs through me. I have always loved you.

And finally, to my great and beautiful spirit family within the Modern Mystery School and King Salomon lineage, those who have come before me and those who have come after: You all have supported me in my path forward. I love you and appreciate you so very much. I am honored to walk this path with you. You are the very best of humanity. Let's create Peace on Earth!

Acknowledgements

I'd like to thank Founder Gudni Gudnason with great honor and respect for sharing deep teachings of Alchemy and magick with me, along with so many aspects of our lineage, for always supporting me, and for EVERYTHING you have done to allow us all to move forward.

I'd also like to thank Ipsissimus Dave Lanyon and Ipsissimus Hideto Nakagome with great honor and respect for their tireless work supporting our mission, truly making this world a better place and, together with Founder Gudni, manning the helm of our lineage toward the North Star as we move forward. You have both helped and supported me tremendously.

I am in boundless gratitude to the Council of Twelve Women who also work tirelessly in steering the helm of our lineage as we move forward. You have all helped and supported me with royal grace and beauty.

I am eternally grateful to Professor Barbara Bullard, M.A., for opening a door that was truly magickal for me, and to Dr. Theresa Bullard-Whyke for ushering me through that door, and being my Guide on this path, when probably no one else could have.

And to Theresa Bullard-Whyke, Ph.D. and Franca Lanyon for being my Alchemy teachers and more importantly, for being such beautiful examples of what it means to be alchemists in your own lives.

Furthermore, this book would not exist if it wasn't for the invaluable guidance, support and encouragement of my literary agent, Ariela Wilcox, a magician in her own right. Speaking of magicians, David Davis, my book cover designer, worked his magick by listening to me explain the image in my head and then making it real.

Advance Praise for The Power of Moving Forward

This an AMAZING story of a Professional Woman who is able to help others through her experiences.

William Fox, MD
Professor of Pediatrics, Children's Hospital of Philadelphia

....

The Power of Moving Forward is a book written for anyone navigating through life's changes. Dr. Carla has created a guidebook using ancient wisdom illuminating the individual stages of life development. Through accessing this same ancient wisdom, she provides guidance on successfully traveling through your individual life course. This book is entertaining, educational, and thought provoking. Whether you feel on top of the world, or are struggling to survive, this book has insights that will inspire you to transform into the person you were truly meant to be.

Mary Tobin, PhD (Holistic Medicine)
Author, "Holistic Healing Power"

....

Within the ordinary life is the raw material for gold. Carla Weis uses her personal story to help us see the potential that exists when a life is honored and excavated for its deep wisdom. As an initiate, she helps to draw the connects between the natural evolution of our life's unfolding and the potential that exists in all of us to reach new levels of spiritual awareness.

How do we become an embodied spiritual being? Who is privileged with this opportunity? Carla Weis demonstrates how the natural unfolding of life can hold all the raw materials for realizing one's true self and purpose. That we are all this privileged; we just need to know how to look.

Whether powerful and miraculous or mundane and commonplace, the eyes with which we look at the foundational material of our life makes all the difference in what we can make from this raw material. Carla Weis uses her life story, told with both simplicity and almost nonchalant introspection to help us see how the truth of who we are is concealed, and then can be revealed and made conscious as we journey through our life. And when and if we are ready, what we can do to bring our raw essence into self-realization.

Kate Siner, PhD (Psychology)
Co-Author with Jack Canfield
Host, Real Answers Podcast
Published in numerous publications including Self and Huffington Post, seen on NBC, ABC, Fox and other major network affiliates

In true autobiographical style, Carla Weis shares her journey of life, self-discovery, alchemical transformation, finding purpose and joy, and even a near death experience. She is a shining example of the power of a can-do attitude, resilience and determination to be victorious, even through the most challenging of circumstances. She highlights the wisdom gained through overcoming trials and successfully navigating the twists and turns, the ups and downs that birth, life, and death bring us all. For anyone looking for inspiration, guidance, hope, and answers to life's most important questions and lessons, allow Carla's journey to guide you to your own insights and illuminate a path forward.

Theresa Bullard-Whyke, PhD (Physics)
Host of *Mystery Teachings* **and** *Quantum Minds TV*
International Teacher, The Modern Mystery School

....

I LOVE this book! As two women neonatologists of different eras, Dr. Weis has been a colleague, mentor, role model, and friend. Her life journey has always fascinated me as well as her ability to get knocked down, bounce back up, finding even more peace from the journey. It is a true gift that Carla is sharing her journey, wisdom, and peaceful spirit in such a well written and easy to read book.

Christine Bixby, MD, FAAP, IBCLC
Division of Neonatology, Children's Hospital of Orange County
Medical Director, CHOC Lactation

Contents

PART ONE – The Matrix

CHAPTER 1

The Alchemy of Being Alive:

CHAPTER 2

The Alchemy of Collapse:

PART TWO – Kindling the Soul

CHAPTER 3

The Alchemy of Moving On:

CHAPTER 4

The Alchemy of Moving into the Light:

PART THREE – Embracing Life

CHAPTER 5

The Alchemy of Being Brought to Your Knees:

CHAPTER 6

The Alchemy of Know Thyself:

CHAPTER 7

The Alchemy of Peace on Earth:

Preface

Why do we read books? What are we looking for? Knowledge? Or just a good distraction from life? Sometimes we just want to be happily entertained and sometimes we are looking for something that will ultimately change our life – even if we're not aware that we're looking for it.

What about this book? Well, since some of it involves my life, you might find it quite entertaining! But my hope and intention is that it can inspire you to change your life, to find what you're looking for. Even if you're not fully aware of it.

Sometimes our soul is seeking, and life gets in the way. Sometimes our heart is hungry, and our mind gets in the way. I invite you to open your heart and your mind and see what you can find somewhere in these pages that might satisfy your soul.

I have lived on this planet for a little over 61 years now. I have five daughters and four grandchildren. I have two ex-husbands. I practiced as an intensive care physician for nearly 30 years. I've studied within a true, ancient lineage mystery school for 12 years. I have developed and adapted to a chronic illness. Some would say that I have a little wisdom to share. But that's not my purpose for writing this book.

My purpose for writing this book is you. I believe in humanity. I know that we all hold divinity and goodness within us. And

I know that with that, we hold the power to create a world of peace. "What?! Have you looked around lately?", you might be thinking. Yes, I have. I understand. Do you want to change that? Or more importantly, do you believe it's possible? I do. And more importantly, I know that the more of us that can shift our beliefs in this direction, it is our collective power that can accomplish this. And always remember that the most important thing to believe in is yourself.

In this book, I have intertwined the concepts of Alchemy in the sharing of my life experiences. I also bring in some Kabbalistic and Hermetic perspectives. My intent is not for all of us to become mystics. We all have our own part to play. But I personally have made these teachings a part of my life. And they have all supported me in rising above the matrix world and making the most of my experience here on Earth. And I really want that for you too. So, by sharing my life experiences in this way, I want to inspire you. I want to do my part in moving us all forward.

Please feel free to read this book however you like. If you're interested in chronic fatigue, or chronic illness of any kind, and you're looking for inspiration, you can just go directly to Chapter 5. If you're mainly interested in knowing more about the Modern Mystery School and deeper life perspectives, turn to Chapter 6. If you really resonate with the idea of world peace, or, like so many of us, you just need a vision of hope, read Chapter 7. And I HOPE you enjoy this book.

Introduction

Have you ever changed your life? Do you still <u>want</u> to change your life? If not, you may not be interested in this book.

I was never content to accept things the way they were. I could often see a better way, a new way, and I liked to ask, "Why?". So, it probably won't surprise you that I became a chemist, a doctor, and a research scientist. But it might surprise you that I also became a wife, a mother of five daughters, and a mystic.

You may be saying, "Sounds like an interesting story....". Well, I guess it is. But perhaps like most people, I've never been particularly eager to tell it. However, for reasons outlined in the Preface, here I am. I will share some of the experiences of my life, the physical and the spiritual. I will have a little fun weaving the concepts of alchemy through the stages of my life with the goal of helping you to see this process of transformation in your own life, and how there is both a science and an art to making changes in our lives and creating the life you want. And how the true path of spirituality, to Know Thyself, will always remind us that we are <u>all</u> of it. And that we can all elevate our minds into the enlightenment that can make this world a better place!

I remember being a happy child, and I have many fond and comforting memories of my childhood in suburban New Jersey during the 1960's and 70's. My parents remained married and in love. I was the firstborn and eventually became the big sister for three younger brothers. I loved dolls and puzzles, books and science, and arts and crafts. I went to Catholic school, my mother took us to church on Sundays, and I always felt connected to God and the angels. I was an early reader, and school and learning came very easy to me. Even after I moved into public school, I continued to excel academically and socially. I was very much influenced by the hippie and peace movement, and women's lib. I graduated high school when I was sixteen because school seemed like such a waste of time, and I wanted to "get on with my life". So, with a small college scholarship, off I went to the local community college. But wait. It wasn't that simple…

Like most mothers of the time, mine was a stay-at-home mom. She was the rock that held it all together. She was always there, kept the house clean and lovely, did the shopping and laundry, prepared all our meals, took care of our needs, could help solve any problem, and always prioritized the health and well-being of us kids. I watched my mother have three more babies, I loved babies and dolls, and I also loved playing and pretending at my father's desk. So being a young woman raised in an era where women rarely prioritized a career over being a homemaker and mother, but also an era that was beginning to present the allure of being an unmarried woman with a job and an apartment of her own, when I finished high school, my aspiration in life was simply to be a medical secretary and have an apartment of my own – and eventually get married and have lots of kids. I certainly didn't want to be in school anymore.

This was very much in conflict with what my father had imagined for my future. He could see so much more for me! At the time, I didn't really understand what the big deal was, but he annoyingly persisted with this idea that I should go to college and get a degree. Suffice it to say, this was a huge turning point in my life. Because of my father's attempts to redirect me, I conceded to register for a medical laboratory technician 2-year degree program at the community college and this seemed to quell my father's passionate concerns.

So, off I went to community college, and guess what? I loved it! It was nothing like high school! I was out in the world. I could choose classes where I was learning what I wanted to learn. I excelled, earned more scholarships, and completed my first college degree. And I wanted more. I transferred to a 4-year Catholic college in Pennsylvania where I lived in a dormitory, selected a combined major of Biology and Chemistry, and completed my Bachelor of Arts degree at the age of 20.

Because my parents did not have the means to pay for my education, I worked full-time as a bench chemist on the night shift and attended classes during the day. When I graduated, I continued working as a chemist. I got married, had my first daughter and after a couple years, I wanted more out of life. I had a new goal. I decided I wanted to get my PhD so that I could work in cancer research and find a cure for cancer. Well, that ultimately led me to attend medical school in Philadelphia during which time I had two more daughters. I then completed a residency in Pediatrics, during which time I had my fourth and fifth daughters. I went on to complete fellowship (subspecialty) training in Neonatal-Perinatal Medicine and found myself coming full circle to be doing medical research in a laboratory while also being a clinical physician in the hospital.

I felt fulfilled as a mother and a doctor/scientist, but there was trouble on the home front. My husband, who had always been very supportive of my career pursuits, wasn't happy. We had grown apart. Shortly after I completed my fellowship training, we separated and ultimately got a divorce.

The children stayed with me, and I found myself a single mother, working 60-80 hours a week as a newly hired doctor. I sought out a different job where I could be home more and still support my children, and I found a new job in Georgia. With my ex-husband's (initial) agreement, I moved to Georgia where I had a wonderful job, a house I loved, and a new man in my life. However, all of this was short-lived due to custody challenges that had arisen. As a result, I moved back to New Jersey so the girls could have time with both of their parents.

The new man who had entered my life was my first spiritual teacher, and we became very close. Since marriage is what you do when you love someone, naturally, I married him. However, I quickly learned that entering a marriage that is the opposite of what didn't work the first time, also may not work. We were divorced after just a couple years.

So, now at age 43, I was twice divorced, had a contentious relationship with the father of my children, and therefore did not have nearly as much time with my children as I would like. I also had debilitating migraines, heavy menstrual blood loss, and was beginning to enter perimenopause. During these years, my daughters were growing up. I did whatever I needed to do to support my children and continued to enjoy being a mother and a doctor. On my own, I was continuing to explore my knowledge of God and spirituality, and I was finding inner peace and joy in my life wherever I could.

As my father always said, "Time changes everything.". It turns out he was right – again. I was beginning to emerge out of this low point in my life. With my eldest daughter now married with a son, and two of her sisters out of high school and two more in high school, I made plans to relocate to California. (Yes, a potential third husband was involved.) About a week or two before we were to leave NJ, I experienced a severe episode of hemorrhaging from my uterus. My daughter forced me to go to the hospital where I was admitted and then went on to die. Wait, what? My near-death experience is not something I have shared with many people. (You can read more about it in Chapter 3.) I had a choice and I'm still here.

About a week or so later, I drove across the country with two of my daughters to Huntington Beach, CA. The rest of them followed shortly thereafter.

I loved living in southern California! I traveled to work in

Hawaii (I know, but somebody's gotta do it) until I got my California medical license. My girls attended high school and college near our home. Life was good.

After about 3 ½ years, I was introduced to a woman named Barbara who almost instantly became one of my best friends. Through her, I learned about a mystery school with a lineage that went back 3,000 years. She told me I should see her daughter, Theresa, to have a "life activation" session (which I'd never heard of before). So, I did receive this life activation session, and I questioned Theresa about this mystery school. I had come a long way on my own, with my first spiritual teacher and my self-study, but I was always looking for anything that could take me further, deeper into my understanding of myself and the universe. I liked how she answered my questions, so I decided to attend a weekend initiation program with her.

Theresa was someone that I could relate to and that had my respect. She was a physicist who was also studying and sharing teachings of spirituality. When I have since reflected on this, it's hard to imagine that I would have trusted anyone else with my time and money, having had more of the latter than the former. But I saw some potential value. Knowledge of God was very important to me. I thought, "Maybe this could take me to my next step, maybe I will learn something new.". And so, it seemed like a relatively small investment to find out. I seized the opportunity. (I like to seize opportunities.)

In that first weekend, I received teachings that I already

understood to be legitimate. That was good for me because it gave me more confidence in the program. I also received teachings that I hadn't heard before. I liked that. I wasn't necessarily accepting them all right on the spot, but I liked having new things to work with.

I continued to explore what the Modern Mystery School had to offer. And I always got something out of it; it always held value for me. I liked that there was a path of progression to follow. (I was very familiar with curriculums.) Honestly, I was really just moving forward on the path until I reached a place where I would realize that there was nothing more for me to gain – until it was no longer worth my time and energy. But that time never came.

At some point I realized that it was all there for me. It was just a question of how far I wanted to go. I kept going and my life kept becoming more fulfilling. I was also able be in service to others on another level, which I always loved and valued. I continued doing work that I loved in a NICU seven minutes from my house. Physical fitness was always an important part of my life, and I had developed an exceptional level of fitness, enjoying body building, kickboxing, hiking, surfing, and martial arts training. My daughters were enjoying the freedom to make of their lives what they wanted.

And then I was faced with the greatest challenge of my life. I discovered that I had a chronic illness. It took me close to four years to realize that there was a diagnostic reason why my brain and my body had been slowly yet steadily deteriorating. I pursued many treatment plans. I could no longer work as a neonatologist and reluctantly retired. It took another couple of years to realize that complete recovery was not possible and that my condition was chronic. I now know that I have a chronic illness, ME/CFS. It cut me at my knees and completely turned my life upside down.

Today I have yet another new life, and what I like to call my "new brain". I have, of course, experimented with every possible treatment option. I used to think that I could overcome anything. That was put to the test. My daily life has been significantly and fundamentally altered, in ways that I could have never imagined, due to my physical limitations.

And yet, because of my extensive training with the Modern Mystery School, and the opportunity this illness gave me to really use it on a deeper level than ever before, I have reconciled with my physical condition. I know this physicality is not who or what I am. It does not define me. And even though it does affect how I am able to physically express myself, it cannot affect my power. I have adapted my life and shifted my state of mind. I have literally risen above what was designed to take me down. And I have more joy and fulfillment in my life than ever before!

Even though I have always had strength, courage and resiliency, there is absolutely no doubt that without my work, study, and training with the Modern Mystery School, and the tools and empowerment that comes with that, my life today would look and feel very different. In fact, it is our physical experiences that can so effectively allow us to move forward in our spiritual progression; to come to Know Thyself in a way that only our physicality can offer.

And so, this book is about being a woman, a mother, and a doctor; about seeking knowledge of God; about healing; about being in service to others; about being a human living life in the physical and progressing spiritually. These are the life experiences that I have.

So please allow me to walk with you along what I hope is an inspiring journey through how life can be good, and life can be bad, and ultimately how it is simply a canvas for us to create whatever we would love it to be – for ourselves and for others. I hope it brings you clarity and insight into your own path. I hope it helps you to take your next step forward. I hope it illuminates the power and goodness that you hold within.

PART ONE:
THE MATRIX

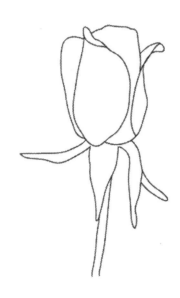

ALCHEMY is simply a process of TRANSFORMATION – a transformation of the self – that happens on all levels of our being. And it begins in a crucible. Life is the crucible.

After each of the seven chapters, I will be introducing the basic process or core essence held within each of the seven stages of alchemy. I will then share "My Experience" - my reflections on how my life experience from each chapter relates to the corresponding alchemical stage. From my reflections, I will also share "My Guidance" for you.

Additionally, understanding that alchemy is about raising our vibration and that music is a form of vibration that can help us do that, I have included a link at the end of each chapter that gives you the opportunity to listen to a song I have chosen to represent the essence of that chapter for me. Maybe you'd like to listen while you're journaling your own reflections from each chapter; there's a page for that too.

"If you want to find the secrets of the universe, think in terms of energy as frequency and vibration."

- Nikola Tesla

CHAPTER 1

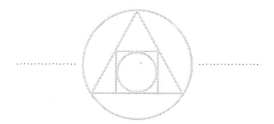

The Alchemy of Being Alive:

Building My Life

Calcination

(Burning away what doesn't serve you)

In this chapter, you will gain insight into the process of finding your way in the world, burning away what doesn't serve you, and allowing your soul to express itself.

Thank you for your interest in my life, and how my reflections upon it may be of some service to you. I was born in New Jersey, a suburb of Philadelphia, under a Virgo sun and an Aries moon, in 1961; I'm Italian on both sides, as they say. My parents had tried for nearly three years to have a child and I was the first. I came two weeks late. My great uncle Jim called my mother every day in those last weeks, excitedly awaiting my birth. My father was away in Fort Dix, NJ training with the army reserves. From the way he tells it, I don't think anyone awaited my birth with more joyful anticipation than he did. Every day, he expected to get called into his commander's office with the news that his wife was in labor and he was being given permission to take leave. When the call finally came, he entered the office with gleeful anticipation, but the news couldn't have been further from what he expected. His beloved stepfather, my great uncle Jim, had suddenly and unexpectedly passed away. And so, my father received his leave and returned home for the funeral. I was born a few days later, bringing joy in the wake of grief, as babies often do.

Welcome to the crucible of my life.

I would ultimately have three younger brothers, being the only daughter. Sometime after the birth of my first younger brother, when I was about four, I began to pray every Sunday in church for God to send me a little sister. But boys kept coming. As it turns out, my prayers <u>were</u> answered, but the answers were delayed by about 15 to 20 years. I would go on to be blessed with five beautiful daughters (no sons), but that part of my story comes later.

I loved being a girl. I loved playing with baby dolls, and I used to ask God, "If I take really good care of my them, will you please turn my dolls into real babies?". I loved pretty clothes and shoes, and I desperately wanted to have long hair, which I was finally permitted to begin growing when I was in first grade. I loved puzzles and card games and science. I had a chemistry set and a magic kit. I also loved wrestling around the floor with my dad, playing sports in the yard and the street, and watching football with my brothers.

I remember when our local gas station (or "service station" as they were called) would reward you with collectible stickers showing the names and pictures of football players, and you could paste them in a book filled with open spaces for all the teams. I loved collecting things – especially putting stickers in books; what kid doesn't? But my father always gave the stickers to my brothers. I told him that I wanted to collect them too. I didn't understand when my father told me that they were for boys. Ah, the beginning of finding my way as a woman in the world of the 1960's and 70's – and beyond.

For most of my childhood, I remember my parents being in love and happy. I felt safe, secure, and loved. My father went to work every day as a claims adjuster for an insurance company and golfed on Saturdays. My mother was always there. Like most mothers of that time, she was a stay-at-home mom, and she took care of everything. She kept the house clean and lovely, did the shopping and laundry, prepared all our meals, took care of everyone's needs, could help solve any problem and fix anything, and always prioritized the health and well-being of us kids. She always read books to me, and she taught me to read when I was about four years old. This set the foundation for my lifelong love of books!

Both of my parents were raised Catholic. My brothers and I were all baptized and received our holy communion and confirmation sacraments. My mother took us to church on Sundays and we received religion classes in a Catholic school.

When I was in kindergarten, I was chosen to be the little girl who would present flowers to the Blessed Mother in the annual May procession ceremony, along with the selected May queen, a girl from the eighth grade. I have always remembered that experience. I was five years old, and I didn't really understand the significance of the whole process. In fact, when my mother was helping me prepare and practice for the ceremony, she kept telling me about how I was going to be carrying the crown for the blessed mother on a pillow. What I <u>heard</u> was that I was going to be carrying a "crayon". That didn't make much sense to me, so one day I asked my mother why I was carrying a crayon for Mother Mary on a pillow. She kindly explained that I would be carrying a "crown", and that it was going to be placed on the head of the Blessed Virgin Mother. My experience during the ceremony became very memorable for me. I remember kneeling before the

Blessed Mother, after giving her flowers, and praying, as I had been told to do. It was the first time I had spoken directly to her. And we had a little conversation. And I loved her. Ever since that day, I have felt a very close connection to the Virgin Mother and, what I now know to be, the Divine Feminine energy.

Fast-forward to when I was nine years old...I witnessed my brother, Jay (who was seven and a half at the time), being hit by a car and thrown down the road. The day before, I had left my bike at school and my parents told me to walk up to the school and bring it home. They instructed Jay to come with me. He brought his bike, walking with me, so we could ride home together. When we came to the only "busy road" (it was one lane each way) that we needed to cross, my younger brother felt that he ought to be protecting me. So, he took charge and said that he was going to walk his bike across first and then come back to walk me across. On his way across with his bike, there was a young man who was making a left turn, and he didn't see Jay and the bike. The car hit Jay, with his bike, and they both went flying.

Watching this, I was completely traumatized, frozen on the sidewalk, and began screaming Jay's name and crying. He remained still and unmoving down the road. Eventually the police and ambulance arrived, Jay was taken away to the hospital and the police drove me home. My very pregnant mother was raking leaves in the side yard. I could hardly wait for the police car to stop before I leapt out and ran for my mother, screaming, "Jay was hit by a car!". I didn't understand why my mother was so calm. The policeman spoke to her, told her what happened and that my brother had been taken to the hospital. Jay was brought home later that day with an injured shoulder and stayed pretty still on the couch.

I was so glad to have him home. I remember the young man who had hit him stopping by the house that day for a visit, feeling so very sorry and remorseful. He apologized to Jay and wanted to know that he was going to be ok. But Jay had his back to him and didn't respond. My mother and I found out later that Jay had really wanted to see him and talk to him, but he couldn't move or roll over because of his shoulder pain. My memory of this experience is two-fold: One of admiration for my brother, for behaving in such a valiant way, and then, a feeling of responsibility for what happened because he was doing it for me. While I soon understood that it was not my fault, I recognized the heart of my brother that day, and ever since, I have revered his actions, done on my behalf, with high honor in my own heart.

Like most kids of that era, I was physically active. I loved gymnastics, bike riding, snow sledding, and exploring in the woods. In the summer, I loved the beach and swimming in the ocean. From the time I was four years old, I took ballet lessons, and I loved it! I continued training until I finished high school, adding in some tap and jazz classes too. (It was after my performance in our annual dance recital, just once a year, that I would be treated to a hot fudge sundae.)

I was an avid reader and loved to learn. I very much enjoyed school, and I always had "straight A"'s. Looking back, it all came very easy to me, and I would love to have been challenged more. The nuns loved me because I could sit still, I listened, obeyed instructions, and, of course, I performed well. (The experience of Catholic school was not as favorable for my brother who can tell you all about how you can use yardsticks and knuckles in the same sentence.)

Beginning in the sixth grade, I made the switch to attend the dreaded "public school". Turns out, it was great. I enjoyed new friends, new teachers, and a different perspective on life. As my school years progressed, I was also beginning to question many religious teachings and to explore other arenas for answers. I continued to excel academically and socially through high school, although I definitely developed the teenage rebellion to authority that started when I was about twelve or thirteen.

As I journeyed through high school, it seemed like such a waste of time to me! There was a whole world out there, and I couldn't wait to immerse myself in it! On the first day of my junior year, I explained to my parents that I had accumulated enough credits to graduate that same year, and I wanted to "get on with my life". After dinner, there was a lengthy discussion around the kitchen table that involved answering questions that, to me, didn't seem very important, like, "What are your plans for after you graduate?". After their customarily calm conversation with me, they reluctantly gave me their permission. I created a plan and at the end of the year, when I was sixteen, I graduated high school.

Of course, this didn't stop me from enjoying those rites of passage like babysitting, school dances, and cheerleading!

Throughout my childhood in the 1960's and 70's, I was very much influenced by the hippie and peace movement, the green movement, and women's lib. As I mentioned, my mother, like most mothers of that time, was what we used to call a "homemaker", literally creating and maintaining a home for the family. And she did it well. But society was moving into an era where women were looking for fulfillment outside the home with a career of their own. There were more young women considering postponing marriage to seek further education. An independent woman with an apartment and career of her own became a cultural icon.

I loved watching TV shows like Marlo Thomas in "That Girl!" and Mary Tyler Moore and Valerie Harper in, "The Mary Tyler Moore Show". I also wanted to be like the go-go girls on "Laugh-In" with their high boots and short dresses. And the hippie movement for peace and love really resonated with me. Why would anyone choose war? I really believed that world peace was possible. I was in sixth grade when the Vietnam war was declared over, and I thought we were close to having peace in the world. [Heavy sigh]

Even though by the time I graduated high school it was becoming more common for women to be employed outside of the home, their roles in the work force were still mainly relegated to those positions considered best suited for women. (It was still quite acceptable for men to call their assistants or secretaries their "girls".) I thought being a secretary would be a really cool job to have! I could have an apartment of my own, wear nice clothes and shoes, and fulfill a role in the world. So, this was my aspiration for my life.

After graduating high school, my parents again brought me to the kitchen table to discuss my plans for the future. There were all manner of pamphlets and catalogs lying on the table. I shared my desire to be a secretary. I loved science and medicine, so it made perfect sense to me that I would attend a 9-month training program and then find a job as a certified medical secretary. (There was a pamphlet for that.) I was certainly done with attending school. It all seemed perfect. I also had a steady boyfriend at the time, and I did want to eventually get married and have babies. (For as long as I can remember, I somehow knew that having babies was a strong soul desire for me, even if I may not have been able to explain it that way.)

Well, my parents didn't seem to share my enthusiasm for my career plans. As usual, they listened and showed respect for my thoughtfulness and my choices, but there was a concerted uneasiness showing on their faces. They calmly began to share their thoughts and feelings. "If you like science and medicine, why not be a doctor?". What?! Like that old guy in the office down the street who has to work around unpleasant odors and touch a bunch of different people all day?! That was <u>not</u> my idea of fun. I liked the idea of greeting people at the front desk, answering the phone, making appointments, filing things and keeping everything organized - not being behind closed doors with sick people.

So, the conversation continued about why I wouldn't consider going to college:

"I don't want to go to school anymore."

"Why not just try it out for a year?"

"It will take too much time. I want to get on with my life."

And so, it went on. Both I and my parents were making an effort to listen and understand, but also each feeling strongly about our own viewpoints. I remember my father being especially passionate, and persistent, in offering alternative suggestions. He saw so much more for me than I could see for myself. He eventually reasoned out loud, "If you're willing to attend a 9-month training program to be a secretary, why not just matriculate into a 2-year degree program at the local college?".

For some reason that I didn't understand at the time, it was important to him that I have a college degree. I saw that the local community college had a degree curriculum for being a medical secretary, and I reluctantly considered it. At this point, I think my father was invigorated from making a little headway, and he pushed for the Medical Laboratory Technician curriculum – also a 2-year degree program. Eventually, I conceded, and the compromise was struck. I would live at home and commute to the local college. I had earned a small scholarship from my high school, and I would work during the summers and in a work-study program at the college to earn money to pay for my education.

Needless to say, this was a huge turning point in my life. Because of my parents' attempts to redirect me, and particularly my father's loving persistence, I went to college...and I loved it! I was so surprised to find that it was nothing like high school! I was out in the world. I was meeting all kinds of people, and they were so much more mature than in high school. I could choose my classes, and I was studying and learning about what I wanted. And as it turned out, the work-study program placed me in the office of the dean's secretary. So how about that? I ended up doing secretarial work! It was a lot of fun, but after a year or so, I realized what my father already knew – it wasn't something I'd be happy doing for the rest of my life.

Before I forget, you'd probably like to know about the time I was hit by a freight train. I was seventeen. The route I used to drive back and forth to the college involved crossing over train tracks. The road had one lane going in each direction. These were the days when very few train tracks had any gate arms. The warning lights would flash for fifteen to twenty minutes before the train actually came past. Drivers had an understanding that you treated the tracks like a continuous yellow light, pausing, looking down the tracks and moving across. The flow of traffic could continue without backing up for miles and miles.

One early evening, I was driving home from school and the red lights at the train track were flashing. All the cars ahead of me were pausing and moving ahead, so I did the same. However, just as I was crossing the track, the traffic light further up the road had turned red, and the cars ahead of me had stopped. There was nowhere to go, and the front of my car was on the tracks. Behind me, a car had also pulled up, unaware that traffic ahead was no longer moving. I motioned for the driver behind me to back up as much as they could so I could back out of the train's path, but she did not understand. I backed up as far as I could, purposefully backing into her car. When I turned around to face forward, I saw the train barreling towards the intersection, horn blaring. Within what seemed like a fast second, my car was suddenly hit, and swung around 45 degrees, parallel to the tracks.

Being a young and inexperienced driver, my main concern was that I had hit the car behind me, especially since I did it on purpose. I immediately got out of the car and went back to make sure that the driver was ok. She was fine but was very angry about her car being hit. (She didn't seem to have any awareness that I had just been hit by the train.) I stayed pretty calm through the whole thing – I mean, after all, I was fine.

When the conductor was finally able to stop the train, and then run all the way back to the intersection, he told me that the impact had knocked a step off the train. We lost the family station wagon that day, but my parents were not at all upset about that; I was alive and intact, and we were all thankful for that. We've always believed that if I had not backed up, even though it wasn't very much, that the outcome would have been quite different. The funniest part of the story comes from one of the many bystanders, who had come out of a local bar. He made sure to tell me, "I saw everything! I saw it all, and you owe me a new pair of underpants!"!

In the summer before college, I had worked doing telephone sales for magazine subscriptions. My first summer after starting college, I shared a summer apartment rental in Sea Isle City, NJ with a few of my high school girlfriends. I loved the freedom, but I also worked three jobs to save money for my tuition. I worked in a little shop making T-shirts and selling souvenirs, I worked on the beach helping my grandfather set up umbrella rentals, and at night, I worked in my aunt's bar as a barmaid. My aunt and uncle's house was attached to the bar. Whenever the police showed up for "disturbances" in the bar, I remember my aunt hiding me in her kitchen because I was not yet 18 (the legal drinking age at the time).

The following summer was spent working in a hospital (the same hospital where I was born) completing the requirements for my associates degree in medical laboratory technology. My fellow students and I performed all the patient blood draws for the hospital every morning. We attended lectures and then worked in the different hospital laboratories during the afternoons.

All things considered, I excelled with my first college experience. I earned more academic scholarships to help pay my tuition, and I completed my first college degree – an Associate of Applied Science (A.A.S.) – when I was eighteen. And I wanted more! I transferred to Immaculata College, a 4-year Catholic, all girl's college in Pennsylvania where my mother, and so many of my female ancestors and elder relatives, had attended. In choosing a major, I couldn't decide between Biology and Chemistry, so I chose both - a combined major of Biology and Chemistry.

By this time, I had bought my first car – a 1972 blue, two-toned, Volkswagen Superbeetle. Since Immaculata, Pennsylvania was a bit far for me to commute, I packed my clothes and belongings from my bedroom into my little Volkswagen to move into a dormitory. I was just a kid, taking the next step on the path I had chosen for myself and not looking back. Without really realizing it, I was driving away from my home and leaving my childhood behind.

I needed to pay for my own tuition, room and board for the next two years, and so I had a plan. A longtime friend of the family held a position of influence in a pharmaceutical company near the college, and he told us they were looking for laboratory help on the night shift. I applied to be a bench chemist and was hired for the 4:00 p.m. to 12:30 a.m. shift, Monday to Friday. So, I attended my required classes and labs during the day, and then rushed off to work by 4:00 p.m. I was an analytical chemist, testing pharmaceuticals. I really loved my work, and I gained new friends and more life experience. And I was able to pay my way through college, including some needed summer classes at Villanova University.

Being at an all-girls Catholic college had its advantages and disadvantages. The nuns made sure I had a hot meal to take with me to work every afternoon. That was really nice. I also received an arts-based education that included philosophy and religion as well as math and science. On the other hand, the dormitories were locked down at 11:00 p.m. (with a chain and padlock). Only the security guards had the keys and they drove around the campus throughout the night. I had, of course, notified the school that I would be returning from work after lockdown every weeknight.

The security guards were made aware of my special arrangement, and they had instructions to let me in when I arrived home. However, there were times, not infrequently, when I would return to my dormitory after work, between 12:30 a.m. and 1:00 a.m., exhausted and needing to be up for an 8:00 am class, only to find that the dormitory door was locked, and security was nowhere to be found. There were times I waited over an hour for them to let me in. I chalked it all up to more life experience.

I was invited into the Sigma Zeta Science and Mathematics Honor Society, and I graduated cum laude with my Bachelor of Arts degree (A.B.) at the age of twenty. After graduation, I decided to continue my employment as a chemist and wait for a day-shift position to open up. There was also my boyfriend, John. Yes, the same boyfriend from when I was in high school.

I was twelve when we met in a movie theatre that my aunt and uncle owned in Sea Isle City, NJ. In the summers, I helped out behind the candy and popcorn stand, and he ran the movie projectors upstairs. We had started dating when I was fifteen, and now that I had graduated college we wanted to move in together. So, we found an apartment midway between his job and mine, in

Norristown, PA, and our life together began. Within a few months, I was pregnant.

We were married in the Catholic church on New Year's Eve, which happened to be a Friday. (My first choice was Saturday, New Year's Day, but since that is a holy day, it was not permitted.) My first daughter, Jaime, was born on the summer solstice, and I loved being a mother! I was able to take three months personal leave from my job in the laboratory. Even though that was very generous for that era, it didn't feel like nearly enough. I became a working, breastfeeding mother with my daughter in daycare. My husband was very supportive and helpful. He even took care of her when he had a weekday off. This wasn't typical for fathers at the time, but as they say, "The times they were a changin'!".

My husband was in the business of water and sewage treatment, and he was beginning to evolve with the industry into computer operations. He liked this field and excelled in this area. He also enjoyed cooking and was good at it. So, we had a deal; he cooked, and I cleaned up. We had our challenges, as any new marriage does, but for the most part, it worked well. And we were happy.

This was the early 1980's and physical fitness was becoming much more mainstream, but not so much during pregnancy. Even so, while I was pregnant, my husband and I worked out regularly in a local gym. Because I maintained this until the end of my pregnancy, the older women at the gym used to joke with me that my baby was going to "come out running!". After she was born, I discovered the "20-minute workout" and continued to work on my physical fitness. I found that my body was never going to be the same as it was before childbirth, but it could be better!

I continued working as a chemist, with Jaime in daycare, and found so much joy in motherhood. My life was full and happy, but after a year or two, I wanted more out of life. I had a new goal. I decided I wanted to get my PhD so that I could work in a laboratory for cancer research and find a cure for cancer.

As I looked into my options, I found a novel and newly established combined MD-PhD program at Temple University in Philadelphia. I figured that if I was going to work in cancer research, I would probably be most effective if I also had an M.D. That's what I wanted – to be as effective as I could. (By this time, I understood the importance of laying a good foundation in order to be set up for success.) I was told that in order to be accepted into the program, I would first have to be accepted into the medical school, since far fewer people were able to overcome that hurdle.

If I was able to complete the first two years of medical school, I would then begin two to three years of PhD work, including my thesis, and then go on to complete my final two years of medical school. So, with this intention, I began my journey to become a medical researcher and to do something meaningful for humanity. I applied to medical school. I still had no intention of practicing medicine.

I did, however, want to have a lot more children. I loved being pregnant (except for the early weeks of morning sickness). I loved being a mother, and, again, I felt deep in my soul that this was an important part of who I was in this life. It was while I was in the process of applying to medical school that I attended some social event with my father. He introduced me to an older woman who was in some position of influence in academics or medicine. She knew I was married with a little girl. I told her of my plans to do medical research and to have more children, and that my husband was very supportive. She said very definitively, and a bit emphatically, that I needed a wife, not a husband. When I politely suggested there was room for discussion in these definitions, she flatly disagreed. And she repeated, "You need a wife, not a husband."

Of course, what she meant was that I needed someone to take care of me while I was on this journey, in a way that only a woman – or a wife – can. She wasn't the only one who shared a similar sentiment. Many people told me I could not be both a doctor and a mother, that I would have to choose between the two. I didn't understand. I wanted to be a doctor and I wanted to have children. What was the big deal? Why couldn't I do both? My mind was made up. They would just have to watch me.

Again, this was the early 1980's. Women were getting accepted to medical school, but there were far more men, and competition widely favored a man. As the summer drew to a close, I had not received any acceptance letters. And so, I set my sights on reapplying for the following year. On the day before medical school orientation was to begin for the new class, which was also my birthday, I received a phone call from the dean of a medical school. He told me that a position in the class had opened up, and he asked me if I was still interested in attending. I responded with an emphatic, "Yes!". And so, on my birthday, 1985, I was accepted into Temple University School of Medicine, class of 1989.

The next day, I went to my work in the lab, gave my resignation, packed up my bench, and bid goodbye to my friends and co-workers. I found it funny that when I said to one of my male co-workers, "I can't believe it! I really didn't think I was going to get accepted!", he replied, "Neither did I.". He was a good friend who supported me, and he knew I was capable, but these were the times we lived in. Not only was I a woman, but I was married, I had been out of school for three years, and I had a two-year-old daughter.

I was very excited to begin this new chapter of my life, and my husband was equally excited at the prospect of his wife being a doctor. We had just bought our first house in Bellmawr, New Jersey, and there was much to look forward to. I commuted on the train and subway between Bellmawr, N.J. and north Philadelphia every day.

My medical school class consisted of about two-thirds to three-quarters men. It didn't matter much to me. I grew up in a house full of boys and I felt right at home. It was more about the excitement of being among academic peers than anybody's gender. I connected with some of the other women in the class, and new friendships began. I told them about my plan to enter the MD-PhD program and ultimately do medical research in the field of cancer. It was not until my second year of medical school that I would have to definitively make up my mind. That's when I could formally matriculate into the combined program.

Many people obviously had doubts about my ability to accomplish my goals, but I did not. I really loved medical school! I was intellectually stimulated and challenged, and I felt like I was doing something purposeful, not just for me but for the world – like I was stepping further into the role that I was supposed to be playing in the world. This was what I had longed for back in high school.

Of course, I also wanted to have more babies. While my husband wasn't as excited as I was about having more children, we eventually agreed to try for another child. I became pregnant towards the end of my first year of medical school. Whitney was born in February of my second year, while I listened to Stevie Nicks and Fleetwood Mac using headphones with my husband's "Walkman" (a portable cassette player), an unusual thing to do during deliveries in the 80's. I took Whitney to class every day, bringing her with me on the trains and sitting with her in the back of the classroom.

I didn't want to disturb any of the other students, and, as it turned out, she was a very good baby. Sometimes the professors would pause briefly, with a quizzical look from the front of the lecture hall, when they thought they heard baby sounds. Eventually everyone knew Whitney was there and she literally became part of our class. I was pleasantly surprised to find that most of the students and professors (not all) loved having a baby in class. They even insisted that her picture be included in our class yearbook when we graduated, and it was!

At this point, I decided that I loved medicine, and I my changed course to simply become a medical doctor. I was able to see so many possibilities for my career beyond medical school that were not limited to, but were beginning to include, practicing medicine.

That summer, I began the grueling clinical rotations, giving us an experience of all areas of medicine, that would continue until our graduation two years later. Working in the hospital most every day and many nights meant that I sometimes missed events like my daughter taking her first steps or birthdays and holidays. All of this tugged dearly at my heart strings, but I knew that I was working to serve the lives of many people, not just my family. My husband continued to be very supportive, helping to care for the children during days while he worked at night. My mother was also incredibly supportive, in fact indispensable, covering those overlapping morning times and overnights, when neither of us were home. As they say, it takes a village.

During my rotation through OB/GYN, I had an ectopic pregnancy, meaning the fetus was growing in my fallopian tube. I began to hemorrhage internally, and nearly died, before I had emergency surgery. As I found out, this is apparently part of medical training – to experience what your patients are going through. (I also had a kidney stone during my nephrology rotation, and my daughter broke her arm during my orthopedics rotation.)

A few months later, I became pregnant again. My third daughter, Nicole, was born in January of my fourth and final year of medical school. By this time, we had hired a nanny to help with the kids. About a week or so after she was born, I was back to work in the hospital for my neurology rotation. I remember the attending physician insisting that we take the stairs everywhere, even though he knew I had just given birth. This was his daily exercise, he told me, and in not so many words, it wasn't up for discussion.

By the time graduation day came, I was still breastfeeding her (as I did for all my children). The venue for our graduating class was the Academy of Music in Philadelphia. From the stage, during the ceremony, I could hear her hungry cry. Unable to tolerate it, I quietly stepped down from my place, surreptitiously left the stage and went to the balcony where my family was sitting. I took her to the bathroom and breastfed her, brought her back to my mother, and quietly returned to my place on the stage. My name was called, and I received my diploma - my M.D. I was 27.

It was time to decide on my specialty for practice, an area of study for my residency training. I had a very hard time deciding between OB/GYN and Pediatrics. I wanted to serve women and children. I was a woman. I had children and loved them. When I shared this vacillation with my assigned counselor, a woman physician, she said, "What about doing Pediatrics and then subspecializing in Neonatology?". I was quick to dismiss it, "Oh no. I could never do that.". (Neonatology is the field of newborn intensive care and includes attending high-risk deliveries and consulting with pregnant women and their families.) At the time, all I understood of neonatology was tiny, sick babies who often died. Ultimately, I chose OB/GYN.

But alas, no one was willing to offer me a position in their residency program. When I had interviewed for these positions (during my last year of medical school), I was a woman, married, and very pregnant with my third child. And I made no apologies about wanting to have more children. So, I guess it's no wonder I didn't get offered a position. With the help of the medical school, we found an opening for a resident physician in a combined program for Internal Medicine and Pediatrics in a prominent Philadelphia hospital, Albert Einstein Medical Center. The first year of the program included some training in obstetrics and gynecology. This sounded like my best choice since I had planned to re-apply for an OB/GYN residency position in the following year. It also gave me more options.

During my first year of training, I suffered through the four months of internal medicine training, I tried to enjoy my two months in obstetrics and gynecology, and ultimately, I very much enjoyed my final six months in Pediatrics - which, by the way, included a significant amount of time working in the neonatal intensive care unit (NICU). As it turns out, a position was open in this Pediatrics residency program, and the medical staff enthusiastically encouraged me to stay and also offered me "no time lost" in the three-year program. I loved the work, and I loved the people. I decided to finish the three-year residency training in Pediatrics and become a pediatrician.

It was during these three years of pediatrics training that I had my fourth and my fifth daughters, Chelsea and Erica. (If you've lost track, that's five kids in eight years, with the four youngest being born in less than five years; I was 30.) You know, it's hard to remember anyone who was happy about my pregnancies - except me. My parents were concerned for my personal well-being. My co-workers were mostly concerned about what would happen to their own workload in the event I needed anything more than our allotted two weeks' vacation per year. ("Oh my God. She's pregnant again." were the words spoken, but they also represented the general mindset.)

There was not yet any form of maternity leave in doctor's training programs, so there was no allocation for workload distribution in the event of a resident doctor being unable to work. I mean, doctors aren't really human, right? They give medical care to other people, but they don't actually ever need medical care themselves. And resident doctors certainly don't have babies. This was pretty much the unspoken understanding. Fortunately for everyone involved, I was always able to work through my pregnancies, have uncomplicated births, and go right back to work.

Well, now it was decision time again. Did I really want to be a practicing pediatrician caring for growing children? I could do that. At the same time, I absolutely loved working in the NICU. I found that I especially thrived in the intensive care setting. I was well-suited for the work. I possessed attention to detail, intellectual aptitude, emotional connection with people, ability to function as part of a team, and was able to take charge while always remaining calm and in control during emergency situations. And I dearly loved the work! But it would require another three years of training to become a neonatologist. Did I really want to do that? Wouldn't it be nice to just go to work as a pediatrician, come home and enjoy my family? Hadn't I trained enough? Hadn't I sacrificed enough?

I finally reasoned that if I began the fellowship training to become a neonatologist and it wasn't working out, I could always quit and practice pediatrics. But if I didn't do the training, I might later regret it. So, keeping my options open, I applied to fellowship (subspecialty) training programs in Neonatal-Perinatal Medicine, and I was accepted at The Children's Hospital of Philadelphia (CHOP), one of – if not *the* - most prestigious children's hospitals in the world.

From the first day of my fellowship, I loved it! I <u>knew</u> I was exactly where I was supposed to be! And that's how it remained throughout my entire career as a neonatologist. All the reasons I couldn't decide between OB/GYN and Pediatrics were completely reconciled here. Mothers, babies, families, operating room, labor and delivery and intensive care management - serving mothers and babies, serving humanity, in fact, saving lives. I found my place in the world.

During my fellowship, we were required to gain experience working in a laboratory and to complete our own published research project relating to neonatology. At CHOP, I had many wonderful opportunities. I decided to accept an invitation from a prominent CHOP neonatologist, who has since become a wonderful, lifelong friend. I joined him on his sabbatical in a well-published pulmonology lab at Temple University Medical School – my alma mater!

As you can probably imagine, I absolutely loved this work! I had come full circle. I was doing medical research in a laboratory, alongside PhD candidates, while also working as an intensive care physician in the hospital taking care of babies. And partnering with some of the most amazing people, I was able to perform and participate in ground-breaking medical research in the field of liquid ventilation and pulmonology, publish many scientific journal articles, co-author textbook chapters, and speak at many scientific conferences in the United States and London.

I felt fulfilled as a woman, a mother, and a doctor/scientist, but there was trouble brewing on the home front.

Calcination

Calcination is the first of the seven stages of Alchemy. Here, we are burning away all that is not really our true essence - burning away the materialistic, the mental constructs, in order to ignite the passion of our soul.

According to Dennis William Hauck in "The Emerald Tablet: Alchemy for Personal Transformation", calcination is a natural process that takes place over time, as we are gradually assaulted and overcome by the trials and tribulations of life.

My Experience:

My experience during this time of my life really was a burning away of mental constructs, societal constructs, religious constructs, and a start to reconnecting with the passion of my soul.

Somehow, I managed to create the life I wanted. I also did not close my mind to alternative ideas. As you have seen, I could reroute myself. But none of this was easy. In the process, I was challenged many times regarding what was more important, the ideas of the outside world or the desires of my soul.

My Guidance:

When your soul's desire calls out, please answer it! Don't let other people's ideas of what you're supposed to be doing thwart your efforts. More importantly, don't let your own mental constructs of what your life is supposed to be create limitations for you. Yes, fulfilling your soul's desire takes effort. It's never easy, but it can certainly be fun - and it is always fulfilling!

Carla's Pearls

"When faced with difficult decisions, choose the option that gives you more options."

"Dream big and be brave."

"If at first you don't succeed, do it like your mother (parents) told you."

SONG

"THE LOGICAL SONG" – Supertramp

https://www.youtube.com/watch?v=kln_bIndDJg

What Did You Learn About Yourself in This Chapter?

[Write about it here]

CHAPTER 2

The Alchemy of Collapse:

My Life Dissolving into Uncertainty

Dissolution

(What's not working and letting it go)

In this chapter, you might relate to the loss that
comes with divorce and single parenting and,
in general, find the insight you need to discover
what's not working in your life and let it go.

Yes, there was trouble brewing on the home front. It began under the surface, as trouble often does.

With my fellowship training complete, I took a position as a neonatologist in a prominent Philadelphia hospital NICU, affiliated with CHOP (Children's Hospital of Philadelphia), and I was finally a full-fledged attending physician with a salary! We were still living in our first home, a three-bedroom twin house in suburban New Jersey, but now we had five daughters. A new house was in order. Yes, that's it. A new house. That's what could make everything better for us.

We needed a school system that could support children who were both academically talented as well as those needing to function in an alternative classroom setting. We found a nice big house in an upscale, charming, tree-lined, western Philadelphia suburb. The kids could easily walk to both the elementary school and a small, local library they would soon love to frequent. Our youngest went to pre-school, one began kindergarten, one first grade, one in third grade, and my oldest attended the middle school.

I was very happy with the support that the school system gave all my children. I loved our new house. I loved my work. But I was working a lot. I had my full-time neonatology position in a busy south Philadelphia NICU. (I say "full-time" but, in those days, there was no such thing as a "part-time" neonatologist, so we actually didn't distinguish between full-time and part-time.) While it could vary somewhat, a hospital neonatologist in my position worked about 80 hours per week, serving in the NICU, the delivery and operating rooms and teaching, and that included 36-hour shifts, with no scheduled breaks for meals or anything else. (Yes, those were the good old days!) And when I wasn't fulfilling my hospital responsibilities, I continued to do neonatal bench research in the pulmonary lab in north Philadelphia.

When I was home, I always tried to make the most of it. I loved being a mother, but my marriage was struggling. My husband, who had always been very supportive of my career pursuits, wasn't happy. I was emotionally growing apart from him, and he was feeling overwhelmed and drained, as you can imagine. This was not what either one of us had signed up for nearly fifteen years before.

In hopes of repairing our marriage, we attended various forms of counseling. Ultimately, we decided it would be best for everyone for my husband to leave. So less than six months after we moved into our new house, he left.

Literally overnight, I found myself a single mom of five girls, aged 4 years to 13 years, and wondering how this was all going to work, but also knowing that I would make sure that it did. I knew that things really were moving in the right direction. Even if, on the surface, it looked like chaos, I knew it was just a temporary disruption.

I found myself needing to play the role of both mother and father. My husband was not in a good place, and he needed to distance himself for a while. Unlike in New Jersey, where my mother, father and other family were nearby, I no longer had this support. The nanny we had in New Jersey had gotten married. So, I hired help and utilized after school programs. My children became latch-key kids. I went through several different nannies and learned that a position caring for five boisterous girls was typically less desirable than, say, a position with two kids, regardless of the pay.

Not wanting to create any more discord than already existed, my husband and I had agreed to use the same divorce lawyer, who also acted as a mediator, and our divorce was finalized after about 2 years.

The girls continued with school, friends, doctor appointments, and birthday parties. Often utterly exhausted when I got home, I would do my best to be present for the girls and their needs, just as much as I had been present for the families that I cared for in the hospital. For the emotional and mental well-being of myself as much as for the girls, I established "Family Days" when we would all spend the entire day together doing something fun, like going shopping, or playing games, or going out to eat. It gave us all something to look forward to, and we created so many wonderful memories. Of course, they didn't always seem "wonderful" at the time. Just imagine taking five girls out to buy new clothes for school!

Ok. I have to tell you the story of the fountain in the mall. On one of these Family Days, we were all out at the local mall in the dead of winter in Pennsylvania. At some point during our outing, we were around the fountain, looking at the coins in the bottom, making wishes and the average folly. My youngest, Erica, who I think was about 4 or 5, was leaning over the edge looking at all the coins and fell into the fountain! Of course, it was shallow, but that didn't change the fact that she was soaked. I immediately retrieved her into my arms and announced to everyone that we needed to go home and began to lead them out. There was a cacophony of objection following behind me.

"Why do we have to go home?!"

"So what if stupid Erica fell in the fountain!"

"I don't care if she's wet!"

I hustled them all out to the car, carrying Erica in her coat to keep her warm, and we made it home in a car filled with a continued commentary of objections.

It's no surprise to most people that a common complaint among siblings is, "That's not fair!". I remember often having to remind them that it doesn't need to be fair. I would explain that I treated each one of them as their behavior and their needs dictated, and I made sure they understood that what was good for one may not necessarily be good for the other.

When pushed, my response was, "This is not a democracy. This is a monarchy, and I am the matriarch.". And, whenever the question came, "Mom, who's your favorite?". Well, the answer is always, "*You* are! You're ALL my favorite!".

Now, I don't mean to portray that there was always peace in the kingdom or that I always had complete command. My God, who could?! There were many moments of pandemonium, and I learned a lot about ruling with love and with boundaries. Their father had ruled with more of an iron fist approach, and I had always been the nurturer. During these years, I learned so much about finding that balance between mercy and justice, that both are needed, and that both come from love. I wanted them to all have the opportunity to express themselves, not just verbally, but also as individuals, so they could grow up to be strong, independent women. Needless to say, it was an adventure!

I always said the escapades that went on in our house on a daily basis could be very successfully televised for everyone's entertainment. Like the times a squirrel got in the house. Or when we discovered that one of my younger daughters was secretly collecting tools from the basement and hiding them under her pillow. Or when two of my daughters who shared a room with a bunkbed decided to split the room into two sections into which the other was not permitted to enter. Little did I know that reality TV like this would soon become an actual thing! In any event, these are just a few of so very many moments that I treasure, and that we can all laugh about today.

At one point, I wanted to give the girls an educational travel experience – and I needed a vacation – so I planned a road trip.

The six of us drove in my minivan from Pennsylvania to Washington, D.C. and Virginia. We saw all the national monuments and a few museums, and we experienced Colonial Williamsburg. (Today, I am fascinated by how much energy I had!)

I remember one night, thinking how nice it would be to take them all out to a fancy Colonial Williamsburg restaurant for dinner. And of course, I was craving a nice night out. I made reservations and when we arrived, the atmosphere was candlelit and quiet with primarily older couples dining. In walks a single mother with her five young daughters, the oldest of which was becoming a rebellious teenager. Well, suffice it to say that the staff did not appreciate all the "fun" we were having. And I use the word "fun" <u>very</u> loosely, because fun is only one of many words that I would use to describe <u>my</u> experience that night.

Over the months and years, we all settled into a rhythm. I kept our traditions, like making apricot strudel at Christmas time, and having Easter socks, and gradually new ones came in. I savored every moment I had with my children. I was fully aware of how fleeting these moments were, even in the bedlam of it all. At one point, I had five girls in three different schools. The mornings were always eventful.

There were even occasional mornings, after a 24-hour shift in the hospital, when I had to leave the hospital, drive home, get them all off to school and then go back to the hospital to finish the day. Sometimes I was doing laundry at 3am because there was no other time to do it. On at least one occasion, I had to bring the girls with me to spend the night in the hospital, staying in my "call room", all following behind me through the halls like little ducklings with their pillows and sleeping bags. But, in spite of all the challenges, I loved it. All of it.

My regular exercise routine that began after Jaime was born, (remember that?) had been abandoned after I started medical school, going on to have four more children in the span of five years. Well, shortly after my husband and I separated, I was able to get back into shape. I discovered Tae Bo, and it served me well. I trained every morning that I was at home, before the girls got up for school. I became very fit again, more fit than I had ever been. In fact, I would continue to train using these workouts for years to come. (I didn't know it at the time, but it prepared me well for the boxing and martial arts that I would begin years later.)

This was the 1990's and only really important people had beepers (like doctors and drug dealers [wink!]), and in a few cases, car phones. It was not unusual for me to be in NICU rounds with the nurses and have my pager go off with a call from one (or more) of my daughters needing to share their "emergency". I usually managed to deal with whatever the situation was calmly and lovingly, but it took time. I was always apologetic to the nurses and a little embarrassed. While I'm sure the nurses were not happy at times, many of them expressed understanding and compassion towards me. They came to find it amusing as they listened to my end of these conversations involving my children's "emergencies".

I was so grateful to them for their understanding and

compassion. I'm sure the irony of my dealing with the perceived emergencies of my children juxtaposed with my dealing with the actual life and death emergencies in the hospital, was not lost on them. I developed many wonderful relationships with different NICU nurses over the years, having shared experiences with them as women, caretakers, healthcare workers, mothers, and often as single mothers.

For the most part, my daughters grew up knowing me as a doctor. Even though as a neonatologist I was a board-certified pediatrician, I still took my children to a pediatrician for routine care and illness when needed. I didn't want to be their doctor. I just wanted to be their mother. The funniest part of all this was that when my children had minor medical complaints, and I gave them medical assessments and/or treatment at home, they would say, "Mommy, I need to see a doctor." I would reply, "I am a doctor." They would scoff and insist, "No, Mommy! I mean a *real* doctor!".

Professionally, I was being invited to present my medical research at various scientific conferences, mostly local, but also across the United States and in London. I was publishing many articles in a variety of scientific journals, and I was co-writing book chapters and other publications for my peers. I was practicing neonatology in a prominent Philadelphia NICU and gaining respect in my field, both from the nursing community as well as my physician peers.

I was living a life that would be hard for most people to comprehend. And I was barely managing. Even though I was clearly capable of very high functioning, I was pushing that to the absolute limits. I wanted and needed, for my children and for myself, to find a way to change it. I had fulfillment with my children and my work, but I dearly wanted more balance in my life. I wanted to be home more; I wanted more sleep. And I wanted to understand more about God and the deeper meaning of it all. Over these years, I had been doing a lot of reading about spirituality and God, beyond religion, and engaging in my own personal study, which, of course, led to more questions.

When the student is ready, the teacher appears.

One Spring, I traveled to New Orleans to present some of my scientific work. On the airport shuttle to my hotel, I heard a few people talking about how no one ever sleeps when they visit New Orleans. Being chronically sleep deprived, I remember laughing to myself. *I* was going to sleep! Of course, the joke was on me.

My life at this point had been completely devoid of any social activity for years. In the past, I had always enjoyed traveling and exploring, and by this point, whenever it happened, it was often by myself. So, my first night there, I walked eagerly into the French Quarter. I loved it! I found the energy and the music and the people invigorating! I don't drink alcohol, but I went in a few bars, had some orange juice, and reveled in the music and general atmosphere. While experiencing new places, I usually prefer to visit the spots where the "locals" like to go, rather than the tourist spots. Consequently, I ventured off Bourbon Street to see what was else was going on in this new place.

I was delighted to discover a wonderfully quaint and perfect little quintessential pool room and bar, with an array of locals. The air was filled with upbeat pop music from the jukebox, the sound of a cue ball cracking into a new rack of billiard balls, and the smell of alcohol and cigarettes. (I don't drink or smoke, but the aroma is unique and always brought me back to those summer nights working in my aunt's bar). At the center of it all was a well-used, coin operated pool table – commonly known as a "pay table". Now, I love to play pool! Back when I was dating my ex-husband, his parents had a pool table, and he had become quite adept at the game. He taught me how to play, and we spent many days and nights on many pool tables!

So, I put my two quarters on the table, next to the line of quarters already there, to secure my turn in line to play the winner. While waiting, I enjoyed watching the guys play and gradually struck up conversation. I had forgotten how much I missed just being out and enjoying myself! I hardly noticed a tall, dark-skinned man standing at the bar across the room.

Soon, my time came to rack the balls and play. I probably won a few games, but I really don't remember. I know that I had a wonderful time and played quite a few games that night. At some point, while leaning up against the wall with my pool cue, waiting for my opponent to take their turn, the tall, black man walked over to me.

He was well-dressed, well-spoken and had a quiet charm. He introduced himself to me, his name was Stefon, and we struck up a conversation. He learned that I was a doctor and I learned that he was a male dancer in a strip club on Bourbon Street, and that he also loved to play pool and liked to come to this bar to play after work; he also didn't drink alcohol. We began to talk about energy. He was someone who could see energy and also had a deep, spiritual understanding that I recognized from my own study. We began to talk about God. My interest in what he had to share was certainly piqued. I went back to my hotel with a matchbook that he had used to write down his name and phone number.

The next day, and every day following, was spent at the scientific conference. But the nights were free. Bill, my very good friend, partner, and mentor, in both the hospital and the lab, made it his mission to ensure that I would have a good time while we were in The Big Easy. So that next night, Bill, several other friends, and I flowed onto Bourbon Street. We enjoyed a great dinner with lively conversation. When Bill found out about my experience the night before, he insisted we go to that strip club. So, we did. As it turned out, Stefon was not working that night, but Bill made sure that we all had a great time! I got very little sleep that night.

The scientific conference continued. As I was moving through the week, I remained quite intrigued by Stefon, and I wanted to have more conversations with him about God. I had come to believe in God from my own direct experience. It began with experiences as a very young child, including my inner connection to the blessed mother. It progressed through my adulthood as my own experiences of life, and of death, strengthened my connection to God through an acknowledgement of a higher power to which I felt very much connected. On my last night in New Orleans, I went back to the pool room. Stefon was there. We played some pool. I told him I wanted to talk more about God. We left and began to walk and talk.

As we walked the streets of New Orleans that night, through and beyond the French Quarter, there was a magick in the air. The streets, lined with their characteristic lamp posts, were wet from a rain shower earlier and all the surrounding light reflected off of them. The air was cool and fresh, and the night sky shone with stars. The words I was hearing from Stefon, who was walking a few steps in front of me as we strolled along, rang with clarity. And then there was the moment. Time actually stopped for me, and I could see the energy of God connecting everything - the energy that was me and everything else. I could see it and feel it. My mind had awakened to a higher dimension than ever before. I had glimpsed, outside of time, the eternal peace and unity of myself as part of everything – and everything was God - and it was absolutely wonderful.

I left New Orleans the following day feeling as if far more than five days had passed. And as the anonymous travelers on my airport shuttle had predicted an eternity before, I had gotten very little sleep. But my life was forever changed.

I kept in touch with Stefon, and we had many long phone conversations. I returned to New Orleans a few times over the coming months as our relationship grew. Stefon seemed to be the exact opposite of my first husband, and I was falling in love.

My life as a single mom of five girls, working too much and not sleeping enough, continued. After four long years of struggling physically and financially, juggling the responsibilities of being a mom, an academic physician, and a scientist, I finally began to hear the words, "Physician, heal thyself". I began to see beyond the mire and entanglement of my day-to-day life into possibilities.

I came to realize that I could seek neonatology positions in other regions of the country where the work standard was different. I didn't need to stay in my current situation. I could change it – for myself and, maybe more importantly, for my daughters. Where we lived, in the northeastern US, it was standard for neonatologists in the higher level academic NICUs where I served, to remain in the hospital during their 36-hour shifts, in addition to regular day shifts. But this was not the case everywhere in the country. For example, in the southeast, it was possible to have a position where your night calls only needed to be 24-hours, and you could take those night calls from home, only going into the hospital when needed.

As a physician, it was an everyday occurrence to receive postcards and letters from recruiting agencies. One day, a mailing came across my desk advertising a neonatologist position in a city in southwestern Georgia. The only reason it didn't end up in the trash with the others was because I recognized the name of the city. It was the city where Stefon had told me he had lived before he moved to Louisiana. I decided to give them a call and get more information about the position. I liked what I heard and agreed to go down for an interview. Once I had opened my mind to the real possibility for a change, I began to contemplate the details of what I had always dreamt of for my children.

I arrived in southwest Georgia for my interview and found that the city and the hospital were very nice. The people were lovely, and the weather was beautiful. It was indeed a much more laid back and slower pace, yet the hospital and the NICU still provided the high-level care I was dedicated to providing. During the interview, which went very well, I mentioned, honestly, that I liked everything I was seeing, but that I really wanted to live near a beach. (I had explored other possible locations near the coast, but they weren't optimal.)

The NICU director said jokingly that he could haul in some sand for me! I liked his enthusiasm, but I also really liked the potential that this position, and the whole situation, could offer for me and the girls. And the coast of both Georgia and the beautiful beaches of the Florida panhandle were not that far away. I was beginning to envision a better life for me and my girls. After raising kids through the cold, ice and snow of winter after winter, the prospect of leaving that all behind was heavenly. I negotiated the position and looked at real estate.

Over these years, my ex-husband had been sorting through his own grief and transition process after our separation and divorce. He needed time and space to regroup and rebuild his life again. From my own experience, I understood the importance of a father's relationship. So, I always encouraged and supported visitation, especially a regular schedule, but he chose not to have that kind of involvement. I could have chosen to hold boundaries around his choice, but I wanted the kids to have any opportunity they could to spend time with him. And so that's how it was.

It took time, but over the years, he would see them more often. By the time I was looking at the possibility of rebuilding our life in Georgia, he had begun having the girls to visit with him at his mother's house, roughly one weekend per month. I knew that I would be able to maintain a similar connection for the girls with him on some negotiated schedule that worked for everyone.

I contacted their father to let him know that I had found a better situation for me and the girls, and to discuss how we could make it work. The result was that he and I disagreed about how to move forward. Now you, as the reader, may not be surprised to hear this. But I was so fixated on moving on, and the logic of it all, that I found myself a bit blindsided.

After some further discussion, I agreed to his proposition that the girls could stay with him in his mother's house until I got settled in Georgia, and once he had a chance to feel better about everything, the girls would come join me in my new home. Well, it wasn't long before I came to learn the facetiousness of his remarks, which had initially been lost on me - or maybe, I just didn't want to believe it.

By the time it all became clear to me, over the next few weeks, I was in my new home and new job, and there were no more discussions about the girls moving. In fact, there was suddenly a custody case.

Here's where I remind you of my purpose for writing this book – inspiration and empowerment – to move forward. So, we're not going to get lost here.

I engaged with the custody case, determined to do what was best for my girls. My oldest daughter, Jaime, was sixteen and she joined me in Georgia a few weeks later, switching schools mid-year. I was able to have the other four girls for their spring break, and we had so much fun! They were also able to live with me for part of the summer, and we were able to enjoy some of the many experiences I had wanted to share with them in this new life. I also was traveling up to New Jersey about every month or so to be with them, while we spent time with my family there. They were also able to visit with me again for some Christmas holiday time. I was so happy that I was getting a chance to enjoy my girls in this new life, albeit in a drastically different way than I had previously envisioned.

I remained in Georgia for a year and a half. I loved the people and my work and made lots of new friends. I was even able to bring some clinical research trials to the NICU. Once I had relocated to Georgia, Stefon did the same, living about 40 miles away where he still had family. So, the two of us were able to spend more time together. (Since we had entered into a relationship, he was no longer working as an "exotic dancer" – just in case you were wondering.)

In the meantime, my ex-husband had built a new relationship of his own, and the two of them had moved together into a house in New Jersey, with our four younger daughters (now ages 9 to 14). Soon after, they were married.

I did my best to negotiate the ordeal of the custody case. Once it became clear to me that the custody issues could not be resolved without further strain on my other daughters, I knew that Jaime and I had to move to NJ where my four younger daughters were now living. I abandoned my efforts and yielded custody. I made special arrangements to continue working in the Georgia hospital, flying down for a long weekend every month, until I could figure out new employment. I sold my house in Georgia and bought a house in NJ, just a few blocks away from their father's house and the girls' schools. I would do whatever I could to be there for them.

Jaime and I arrived in our new home just days before 9/11.

Dissolution

In the second stage of Alchemy, Dissolution, we are letting go. It's becoming clear that certain situations or people are no longer supportive, or simply no longer exist, and as we let go, seeds of something new are being planted. But first, the old needs to be washed away and we need to let it go.

My Experience:

I had preconceived notions of how my life could be and I wanted to hold onto that, but I had to realize that it wasn't working. This was true for me in several cases: In my first marriage; in the resulting situation of struggling as a doctor and a single mom; and in my new life in Georgia. Only after seeing what's not working, <u>and</u> being willing to let it go, could something new come in. This is all part of moving forward.

Clearly, my life was out of balance. It's no coincidence that I was beginning to explore spirituality; my soul knew that I needed spirituality in my life to have balance, and it was calling out for healing. Fortunately, I listened.

I also experienced that when old systems are falling apart, and new ones haven't yet taken hold, sometimes it's difficult to see things clearly - especially when we haven't been able to fully let go. Without that clarity, it's hard for us to make decisions that are sound and that support our vision to move forward.

My Guidance:

Know when things are not working, and when you need to allow certain situations, or people, in your life to dissolve out of it.

Be open to new ideas and different ways of doing things that can still support your soul's calling. It's better to make a change, to live and learn, than to remain stuck in situations, or in emotions, or in mental constructs.

Do your best to stay clear-minded as much as possible. Meditation helps with this. Be open to welcoming the balance that spirituality, and a spiritual practice, will bring into your life.

Finally, it doesn't do anyone any good to get stuck in blaming others for why things aren't different or better for you. Let it go. Always focus on what <u>you</u> can do to move yourself forward.

Carla's Pearls

"Live and learn. Letting go is part of living."

"We are both physical and spiritual. We need to care for both."

When you don't like how a person behaves and you know it is their pattern, instead of complaining, ask yourself this question:

"What did I expect?"

It will save you a lot of emotional turmoil.

SONG

"THE RAIN SONG" – Led Zeppelin

https://www.youtube.com/watch?v=TRt4hQs3nH0

What Did You Learn About Yourself in This Chapter?

[Write about it here]

PART TWO:

KINDLING THE SOUL

CHAPTER 3

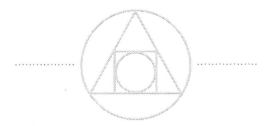

The Alchemy of Moving On:

Reorganizing My Life

Separation

(Rediscovering yourself)

In this chapter, you will find insight into the process of re-creating your life, discovering the best parts of yourself, and realizing that you don't have to be alone.

Jaime and I arrived in New Jersey just days before 9/11. My TV cable installation was not fully complete, and so I watched a snowy TV screen, with the picture fading in and out, while listening to commentary of the events that were unfolding on that historic morning. I felt the fear and uncertainty of what the future held for the world. I wanted to have my children with me. I wanted to hug them. I didn't know what they were hearing in school, and I wanted to make sure they had support in processing what was happening. The school sent them home early. After they got to their (other) home, I was eventually able to speak with them on the phone and I felt a little better.

Within days of when the commercial airlines resumed their flights, I was on a plane headed to Georgia to work. I had never been, and have since never been, on such an empty plane – about five passengers on the entire plane. The world was changing. Everyone could feel it. And my life was certainly changing.

Shortly before I moved from Georgia, Stefon and I had decided to get married. At some point after I relocated to New Jersey, he was able to come and move in with me. We planned for a spring wedding.

Except for the week I was working in Georgia every month, my days were my own. I was getting back to myself. I loved my new house and was really savoring it. My daughter, Jaime, and I planted flowers and enjoyed making a new home. I continued to explore my spirituality, on my own and with Stefon, and I was feeling more balanced. Jaime had me all to herself and was attending the local community college with an interest in law and criminology. I spent as much time as I could with the other girls.

Erica, my youngest, came to visit with me every day after school. I helped with her homework and was happy to be able to connect with her on a regular basis. I was gradually getting back to connecting with all my younger girls on a much more regular basis. And all five of them were finally back together in one town!

At the elementary school, I became a room mother! That was something I had never been able to do before, and it was great. I was able to participate in school activities with the girls. I have always loved celebrating the holidays with the girls, and I could be involved with that not just at home, but in the classroom. And of course, I just love all kids!

My wedding day came. All my daughters were in the wedding, and they looked so beautiful! I had a new life and a new husband, and my hopes were high for the future. I continued to travel to Georgia for work, but also began looking into more local positions.

I found out that the academic hospital where I had completed my Pediatric residency in north Philadelphia had a new chairman and a changing structure. They were now hiring traveling neonatologists, known as "locum tenens", to fly in for weekend coverage. (Yes, the world was changing.) I reached out and scheduled an interview.

During my visit, it was like Old Home Week! Almost all the same nurses from the days of my residency ten years before were still there! It was great fun reconnecting with everyone. And the new chairman was such a nice guy. He appreciated my new situation and was thrilled with the opportunity to have me covering the NICU. So, we agreed on my contract to cover the neonatal and perinatal responsibilities for the hospital over an in-hospital weekend, Friday to Monday, once or twice a month.

I took on this role and enjoyed being back in an academic environment without all the time commitment and stress – beyond the typical stress of the work itself. I loved doing what I was good at – caring for babies and families in the NICU and the delivery room, leading bedside management rounds and teaching the residents and fellows. I felt like the prodigal son – or daughter - returned. And I still had the time I treasured to be available for my growing daughters.

I haven't shared much, so far, about what it's like to be a neonatologist - to work as an intensive care doctor caring for babies and their parents. If at some point you've had a child in the NICU, you've had a glimpse.

When you walk into a NICU, it is quiet and clean; there is a sense of reverence for the innocent life that fills the space. Sometimes it is well-lit, and sometimes the lights are dimmed. The patients in the NICU are newborns and are often found inside individual, enclosed, self-contained environments created by plastic isolettes. These newborns have often been born prematurely, but not necessarily.

Maybe they have had a challenging experience while they were in the womb due to a pregnancy complication, or maybe they have had a delivery into the world that threatened their life. Sometimes they have been born with some known or unknown, seen or unseen, abnormality, genetic or otherwise. They may weigh less than a pound or more than ten pounds. You may see a barrage of life supporting equipment surrounding their isolette, or they may be swaddled in blankets sleeping quietly in a small crib.

When I first became a mother, I had no idea that there were places like NICUs. My understanding of birth was that either the baby survived and was healthy or it didn't. I was unaware of anything in between. In the world today, most people have heard of NICUs and have some understanding of the issues that can arise for babies around the time of delivery. Because the field has expanded so much, many people know someone who has worked in a NICU, or had a child in a NICU, or been a *patient* in a NICU!

With the technological progress that has been made over the second half of the 20th century (before that time, neonatology did not exist), we are able to support the life of very small, very premature, and very sick babies. There are often ethical issues that arise, but those go beyond the scope of this book. Suffice it to say that we can literally perform miracles in saving the lives, and hopefully the well-being, of very small and very sick babies.

As neonatologists, our responsibilities are active around the clock, with no scheduled breaks. Shifts can vary from 10 hours to over 24 hours and have typically been in the 24-hour ballpark. Usually as a solo doctor, along with all the NICU nurses and respiratory therapists, we are responsible for the care and well-being of all the babies in the NICU. We also cover any high-risk situation in the delivery room, being present for every high-risk delivery and every cesarean section delivery in the operating room. It is our duty to be present and assume care of the baby from the very moment they are brought forth into this world.

We are also responsible for any "healthy" newborns who, at any point, develop life-threatening complications while they're still in the hospital, or whenever their pediatrician may request assistance or consultation for the baby's care. We also make ourselves available to speak with parents-to-be in the Labor & Delivery unit when there are complications to the pregnancy or the labor that may affect the baby. Additionally, we are available for the occasional situation that may show up in the hospital's emergency room involving a delivery or a newborn, or sometimes a critically ill child.

So, as you can imagine, emergencies are a daily (and nightly) occurrence. There are also technical responsibilities like placing a breathing tube into the airway of a tiny baby to support their breathing, placing special intravenous (IV) and arterial lines that can remain in place for long periods of time (sometimes into the umbilical cord), supervising ventilator (breathing machine) management, and deciphering x-rays and blood tests in the midst of an emergency. Moreover, speaking with mothers and fathers, and often other family members, about the critical care of their child is an integral part of our responsibilities. We have the hallowed duty of communicating information to them regarding decisions that can vastly affect the life of their child, and sometimes about the death of their child. This gives you some perspective into the life of a neonatologist, a career that spanned nearly 30 years of my life.

Yes, this work has been very stressful and consuming, but it has also been extraordinarily fulfilling! I will never be able to do justice in sharing my experiences of having parents thank me for saving their child's life, or altering the course of their child's outcome, or supporting them through their indescribable grief during the process of losing their child. Nor would I be able to adequately describe the absolute honor of being able to assist babies during their precious entry into this world with comfort and protection, and also in assisting babies during their departure from this world with comfort and dignity. Or the feeling of being able to bring comfort, healing, and relief to so many babies and their parents, both in labor, during delivery, and in the NICU.

Now, I'd like to bring you back to my experience of returning to work in this particular Philadelphia NICU. There was one particular moment that I have always remembered from working in that NICU during that time, and it didn't have anything to do with my work. I was chatting with one of the resident doctors who was asking about my family situation. She looked at me with a knowing look in her eyes and then told me a story. It was the story of how King Salomon the Wise had settled a dispute between two mothers who were each claiming to be the mother of a baby. His solution was to tell the two women that the child would be cut in half so that they could each have half. When the real mother cried out and yielded the baby to the other woman, King Salomon knew she was the real mother, and he gave her the child. The resident who was sharing the story told me that I was that mother because I had been willing to let my children go so that they wouldn't have to suffer. I had never heard that story before, and I just silently cried.

After a while, two of my younger daughters, Nicole (13) and Chelsea (12), were able to move back with us, joining their sister Jaime. I was getting my family back.

Stefon was occasionally traveling up to Massachusetts to spend time with his daughter from a previous relationship. When he was home, we continued to enjoy our time together, but I was beginning to see the patterning and identities that I still held within me regarding marriage from my Catholic, and the general societal upbringing. Stefon had brought things into my life that greatly supported me, we enjoyed each other's company, and I loved him. So, it naturally followed for me that I would marry him and live happily ever after. Wasn't that what you were supposed to do? Well, I was learning otherwise. I was becoming aware that I wasn't happy in our marriage, even though I very much respected and appreciated the role he played in my life.

We had been married about two years when we separated. Our divorce was final a couple years later. We always respected each other and had been able to communicate well through it all. Our relationship had always been amicable and that didn't change with our divorce.

I did whatever I needed to do to support my children and continued to enjoy being a mother and a doctor. With the spiritual foundation I received from my time with Stefon, I was continuing on my own to further explore knowledge and understanding of God and spirituality. I had always been someone who was able to see the beauty in life and make the best of situations. And now, despite life's ongoing challenges, I was finding even more inner peace and joy in my life. And I continued to be militant with my physical fitness.

After so many years of working out at home, using various fitness strategies, primarily cardio-kickboxing, I found my way to a gym. Jaime and her boyfriend had bought a gym membership and told me I would like it. So off I went to see what this gym experience had to offer me. As is typical, I had a consultation with one of the trainers.

She did my intake and asked me about my fitness goals. Well, I hadn't really ever thought much about fitness goals; I always just focused on getting better than I was before, as fast as I could. In an effort to answer her question, the only thing I could think of was how uncomfortable it was to do cardio when I was pushing myself to my limits. I thought maybe she had some way of training that would make that easier. So, I said, "I'd like to get better at Cardio." She proceeded to add <u>another</u> 20 minutes of cardio to the workouts she had prepared for me. I was a bit annoyed and disappointed. I was thinking, "I don't want to <u>do</u> more cardio; I just want to be <u>better</u> at cardio!". Well, I did what she recommended, and I *did* become more proficient at cardio training when I embraced it.

Now, this was at the beginning of the century. I realize there are more contemporary and varied approaches to cardiovascular fitness today, but this experience became a life lesson for me: If you want to get better at something, generally speaking, you have to do <u>more</u> of it! There are no short cuts to avoid doing uncomfortable things if they are part of your path forward. I have found that, usually, when things are uncomfortable, there is an opportunity for improvement, for growth. When I find that pushing myself is uncomfortable, I know I'm doing it right. Challenging myself has always resulted in a learning experience; it has always helped me on the path to know myself. The challenge is always about me facing myself. (In boxing, we sometimes train in front of a mirror, making this lesson very literal.)

My youngest brother, Michael, had competed in the sport of bodybuilding since he was fourteen, and he was on his way to becoming a professional bodybuilder. (He has since turned "pro" and competed in the Mr. Olympia competition.) Now that I was working out in a gym, I was using all the equipment and I loved weightlifting! (Maybe it runs in our genes.) Anyway, my brother gave me a few pointers, eventually created workouts for me, and generally guided me with my progressing workouts and dietary management. I had become a bodybuilder, competing with myself. I was also taking fitness classes and learning to box, which became another favorite for me!

I have learned that any fitness regime will teach us about ourselves, and about life in general. We learn about balance and discipline, self-awareness, and transformation. Bodybuilding in particular, brought me to my next level with all of these virtues. I became tuned into my body to an even finer degree than before. On a much deeper level, I was paying attention to my body; I was able to listen to my body and know it's needs and its limits. All of this fine tuning came from my experience - taking myself a little too far in one direction or the other, and then having to dial it in a little better. I learned so much about myself – not just about my physical body, but also about my mind and my spirit. In fact, it is our physical experiences that can so effectively allow us to move forward in our spiritual progression, to come to Know Thyself in a way that only our physicality can offer.

In fitness, we're always focused on our next goal, our next refinement, our next challenge to tackle. That's how we transform. This book is about the power of moving forward, and when we move forward, we transform – ourselves and our lives. And in that transformation, we find our power.

Muhammad Ali said: "My wealth is in my knowledge of self, love, and spirituality."

Rocky Balboa said: "Going one more round when you don't think you can. That's what makes all the difference in your life."

[If you're a fitness fan, you'll want to read my website blog on bodybuilding and spirituality (link found in the Resources section).]

Our body is our temple and taking care of it is important. I invite and encourage you to explore the possibilities that exist for your own personal, physical, and metaphysical, transformation. The building and refining of your body can lead to the evolution of your soul and spirit – if you let it.

Ok, back to my story. While my level of physical fitness continued to upgrade, my physical health in general had some issues. (Incidentally, so did my house. The basement had developed extensive mold. Having grown up in the northeast, I was used to that. But I had no idea, at the time, what the implications of all this would be for my future health. More on that later.)

I had been having debilitating migraines since before I moved to Georgia (way back in Pennsylvania), and they were continuing. I was also experiencing heavy menstrual blood loss. I was chronically anemic. There were several times that I needed to go to the hospital for blood transfusions. It seemed my female hormones were shifting. I was beginning to enter perimenopause. And my daughters were growing up.

As they say, children generally do what we *do*, not what we *say*. So, at the age of twenty, Jaime decided to get married. The following year, at the age of forty-two, I became a grandmother.

What a joy! I remember in earlier years being told by many nurses how wonderful it was to be a grandmother, but I really didn't believe it could be as wonderful as they were saying. How could anything be better than being a mother? I couldn't comprehend that possibility. Well, my own experience brought me to a new realization. Being a grandmother really does bring another level of the joy that comes from motherhood!

By this time, we were several years into the 21st century. I was being nudged and encouraged to try a new on-line dating site and go out on some dates. Since the website purported to connect you with compatible mates, it sounded like just what I needed. (Looking back, it's clear to me that I still hadn't healed whatever I needed to heal around my ideas of marriage.) Anyway, the good news is that I hadn't given up on love!

You may not believe it (or maybe you will), but at this point I found potential husband number three. Through this compatibility website, I met a guy, Kurt, who did seem very compatible with me. We began connecting via email and then talking on the phone. Kurt was an American working in Europe but had been planning to request a transfer to Honolulu. He had traveled a lot for work and was ready to settle down. After the better part of a year, we felt ready to make a commitment to each other. He asked how me, and the girls would feel about relocating to Hawaii, so I asked them. They were ready!

Kurt's transfer wasn't due for a while and the timing was uncertain. Never afraid to jump into a new life adventure, I began to make plans for employment in Honolulu. Kurt and I talked about finding an interim place to live in California, where we could begin to make our transition to our Hawaiian life, and I could travel from there to Hawaii for work until our move was complete.

Kurt and I spent some time in southern California looking at real estate in a few areas northeast of Los Angeles, where we thought it would be nice to live and also support the further education of my youngest daughters. I explored a neonatology position in an academic women and children's hospital in Honolulu. Eventually, I went for an interview, and negotiated a position where I could travel in from California for seven to ten days every month, covering night shifts for them. They expected, as did I, that my move to California would be within several months.

I was beginning to emerge out of this low point in my life. Jaime was married with a son of her own. Of the other four girls, Whitney and Nicole had graduated high school and Chelsea and Erica were in high school. Whitney, Nicole, and Chelsea had now been living with me. Erica was the only one still living with her father.

Kurt's transfer out of Europe was being delayed month after month, still with an uncertain time frame, and the hospital in Honolulu was anxiously waiting for me to fill their needs. I decided to make my own plans to relocate us to southern California. I had moved myself forward in my own spiritual exploration and my mind was expanding. I realized even more that I could move wherever I wanted! I could create whatever life I chose. Having grown up, then raised my own children, through the northeast winters, I'd really had enough of the cold, ice, and snow. (As you know, I had always loved the beach.) And being chronically anemic now, I was much less tolerant of the cold weather. I found Huntington Beach on a map of southern California, and it just felt right.

Unsure if this was an area in which I would be staying, I contacted a local California realtor about a house rental. I flew out to Huntington Beach and looked at some houses for me and the girls who were living with me. I secured a darling house on a quiet street near the beach, with plenty of room for all of us. I found a buyer for my New Jersey house. (Kurt was aware of all of this, and we still hoped that our plans to be together would materialize.) Whitney wanted to continue attending the local New Jersey college and would move into a nearby apartment. Nicole, Chelsea, and I made our plans to drive across the country. My youngest, Erica, now 14, was the only one still living with her father, and it was agreed that she would stay there for the time being. Jaime and her family decided they would move out a few weeks after us.

About a week or two before we were to leave NJ, with most of our belongings packed up, I experienced a severe episode of hemorrhaging from my uterus. Over the years, I was accustomed to very heavy bleeding every month; some months were worse than others. But this time, it just wouldn't stop. No matter what I did, the blood just kept coming. I did my best to control the flow and figured it would eventually stop. (In the hospital, as a medical student doing my surgical rotation, we learned that, grimly, "all bleeding eventually stops". I wasn't thinking about this at the time.)

I ended up just sitting on the toilet, crying. Whitney was the only one at home and she found me there. When she asked what was wrong, I told her that the bleeding just wouldn't stop. She said she was taking me to the hospital, but I refused to go. Being a good doctor, I was, naturally, a very bad patient. I didn't want to go to the hospital. What were they going to do that I couldn't do? (See. Very bad patient.) She quite stubbornly insisted, not taking no for an answer, and coerced and compelled me into the car. The reality was, I probably could have convinced any one of my other daughters that I would be OK and to just leave me alone. But not Whitney. She was the only one who could've taken that bold action against my wishes – thank God – and she did.

She forced me out of the house and to the hospital. After spending the rest of the night in the emergency room, I was finally admitted to a bed in the hospital. My room was on a general medical-surgical floor, at the very end of the hall, furthest away from the nurse's station. Whitney had stayed by my side all night in the emergency room. Once I was settled into my room, I assured her it was fine for her to go home and get some rest.

It wasn't long before I realized that I wasn't doing very well. I was continuing to bleed at a steady pace, and I didn't feel well at all. I mustered all my energy, which was very little, to send a brief text message to Jaime. She, her husband, and a couple of her sisters were an hour or two away at my brother's Jersey shore house. I wanted to let them know what was happening. They immediately left the shore and drove up to the hospital.

By the time they got there, I had been working very hard to stay conscious. They called the nurse into my room, who was trying desperately to get my blood pressure and find a vein for another IV. I heard her mutter that I belonged in the intensive care unit.

In the long hours before, while I was trying to stay conscious, I was very aware that what I was actually doing was trying to stay alive. I could sense a circumferential rumbling, a "loud" rolling vibration, that was coming up from my feet and rising up my legs. I knew, if it was allowed to continue, it would take my life. I needed to keep it abated. I worked very hard, for hours, to keep it from moving up. I somehow knew, even with all my effort, that if that sensation made it up to my chest, there would be no controlling it and it would take my life.

My daughters surrounded my bed. They held my hand and spoke to me encouragingly. They didn't know anything about what I was feeling; I could hardly talk at all. But they knew it was a life-or-death situation. They said, "Don't go into the light, Mom!".

Eventually, I could feel the rumbling vibration moving up to my abdomen, and I knew that I could no longer stop it from reaching my chest. I told them that I was leaving. The nurse asked them all to exit the room. Of course, they didn't want to, but they slowly and begrudgingly went into the hallway, not wanting to interfere with my treatment. But Nicole stayed, holding my hand, telling me not to go into the light.

I knew that I was leaving my body. I could feel it. The vibration was reaching my chest and I had no control over it. In the outside world, I'm told that my eyes rolled back in my head, I vomited into my throat, became still, and the nurse could not find my pulse. In <u>my</u> consciousness, I had traveled to another place.

I found myself standing in complete and absolute darkness. Even though I couldn't see anything but blackness, I was aware that my feet were standing on a precipice, the edge of a seemingly eternal abyss. I was very aware that I had left my body, and that I could continue, moving off that edge, to fly out into the beyond, and learn things that I desperately wanted to learn. I knew I would be OK; somehow that was being communicated to me. I also knew that there was no guarantee that I could come back to my life; I might be able to, and I might not. I had a choice to make. In a moment of uncertainty, I thought of my daughters. I turned my head back around to see them once more.

As I turned my head around and "saw" Nicole and her sisters, I was immediately back in my body. I felt the vomit in the back of my throat, I coughed, and I was aware of the nurse's voice. And of Nicole, still standing there, holding my hand.

My near-death experience is not something I have shared with very many people. In fact, I didn't share it with anyone, other than my daughters for many years. Even now, as I write this, it feels strange, like I am sharing something very personal, very intimate, very...well, secret...that isn't meant to be shared. (I'm secretly hoping that people will just skip reading this chapter.) But

I decided to document my experience here, in hopes that it will somehow help other people in their own journey.

Over the next day or two, I received blood transfusions and intravenous fluids. It continued to be very difficult for me to stay in my body – to stay alive. I was not moving or talking, but I was exerting incredible mental effort to stay alive – to stay in my body. I could have very easily just "let go". But I didn't. I wanted to stay.

I ended up having emergent surgery to stop my uterus from ever bleeding again (no more children for me), and a large fibroid, that somehow was never seen on ultrasound, was removed. After the better part of a week, I was discharged home to recover.

Determined to keep our cross-country schedule, about a week later, I drove across the country with Nicole and Chelsea to our new home in Huntington Beach, CA. It felt so good to just hit the road and breathe! We had a date when we were expected to arrive in our new house, but I had planned for our schedule to be relaxed. We had time to stop along the way and experience the country and see so many places we had never been before. We had so much fun!

One of the many places we enjoyed was Texas. While we were there, we went into a shop where the girls decided to buy themselves some cowboy boots. The young man was very friendly (I'm sure it had nothing to do with my two beautiful, young daughters), and he invited us to stay in town that night for a big rodeo event that was happening. We had never been to a rodeo before. So, we stayed, and we had a blast! The people were all so nice and welcomed us with open arms and open hearts. But then we needed to move on. We watched the sunrise at the Grand Canyon - so perfectly beautiful! We went on to enjoy spending time at the Four Corners, and then in Las Vegas.

We finally made our way to Huntington Beach and into our new home. This time, I had created my new life, from my own sense of a cultivated and balanced self, and I welcomed it! Hello California!

Separation

In the third stage of Alchemy, Separation, we are separating out the best parts of who we are, our heart and soul. It is a conscious rediscovery of our true essence; we are choosing what that is and leaving the rest behind. Then, we have something to work with and we can move forward, with a clear vision.

It's also a time where we may realize that we don't have to do everything alone anymore. We are recreating our internal structure which allows for more of a sense of unity.

My Experience:

In this section of my life, I had to pick up the pieces of my life, and yet there were still things within myself that I needed to recognize as not helpful and leave them behind. I completely shifted my lifestyle, and I experienced my second divorce. In all of this, I was getting closer to finding myself.

I had always felt like I needed to do everything myself, like I was navigating my life alone. Even though I had many people in my life, I always felt like I was a lone ranger on a mission, stragglers be damned. Once I realized that my only competition was myself, that it was just me facing myself, I could get closer to knowing myself on a higher level, beyond the physical, and I was more relaxed. I felt more connected to my true essence and therefore more connected to the world around me and the people in it.

I also had a near-death experience. Of course, near-death experiences are the ultimate Separation - of our spirit essence from our physicality.

My Guidance:

Divorce, or any major separation, is not to be minimized. It really is a grief process and a significant transition in life; it takes time. Of course, everyone experiences it differently, but there has to be room for personal healing. No matter what the circumstances, it always brings with it an opportunity for healing and personal progression. Take the time. Give yourself the time.

If you're feeling alone, maybe it's a time to realize that it doesn't have to be that way. You can control that. Explore what belief systems or identities you might be holding onto that are keeping you alone. Sometimes we need to be alone. Other times when we feel alone, we may be keeping ourselves separate. Find out what within you might be keeping you from who and what you really are, in your heart and soul. Find that which is good within you, and you will begin to see that goodness around you.

Train your body to find out who you are, beyond your body.

With regard to near-death experiences, I don't recommend them. Do whatever you can to stay alive. You don't need to die to learn how to live!

Carla's Pearls

"Treasure every moment."

"Give yourself time to heal."

"My only competition is myself."

"When you feel like you can't do any more, do one more rep for me."

....

SONG

"GONNA FLY NOW" – Rocky Orchestra (music by Bill Conti)
https://www.youtube.com/watch?v=LOyHMftfbGA

What Did You Learn About Yourself from This Chapter?

[Write about it here]

CHAPTER 4

The Alchemy of Moving into the Light:

Finding a Path and a Guide

Conjunction

(Healing and harmonizing)

In this chapter, you will gain insight into your own spiritual evolution, the empowerment that comes with true healing and a unification with yourself, and how to find some sense of harmony in your life.

We now had a new life in southern California! It was sunny and warm every day! I loved it! The people everywhere also seemed sunny. They were all friendly and seemed to have a calm happiness about them that was strikingly different than the northeastern U.S., but also somehow different than the southeastern U.S. as well.

After a week or two of getting settled, I was off to Honolulu for my first stint of work in the hospital there. In Hawaii, there was yet another culture of people within which I could be immersed. I really enjoyed getting to experience the way different regions of people had different ways of living. There's always so much we can learn. (It's always been amazing to me that we can all be so different, and yet, we are all so much the same.)

The hospital was very busy! My time there was quite stressful, and the hours were long, but I thrived on that. And I loved being able to provide the services that I was so well-trained to do for the babies and their families. Everyone I worked with in the hospital were stellar humans. We were a good team.

My daughter Nicole, having recently graduated high school, was getting matriculated into the local college. Chelsea was getting registered for the local high school, to begin her junior year.

After about a month or so, Jaime and her family arrived. They stayed with us for a while until they could get themselves situated. And then Erica came, ready for her sophomore year of high school.

It wasn't long before Whitney moved too and continued her college education in California. My house was full of family again!

Even though my "home" had aways been in the New Jersey and Philadelphia area, I felt very much at home in Huntington Beach. I loved that I was no longer the atypical person who was smiling and saying hello to people. Everybody was doing it! In general, there seemed to be a more open-minded approach to life, a willingness to explore ideas and different approaches. This was a welcome change for me. In my experience with the scientific community, there was plenty of willingness to explore new ideas and approaches – that's what we did! But outside of the scientific community, I had not found a generalized acceptance of thinking outside the box. So, I found my experience of southern California refreshing.

After about a year or so of traveling back and forth to Hawaii and communicating with Kurt, it became clear that our relationship was not going to move forward. I had to reconcile, within myself, yet another "failed" relationship. I would never give up on love, but I was gradually learning about myself – and refining myself. I was coming to feel more whole and empowered within myself as a single woman.

Over the ensuing years, the girls were living their lives and having their own experiences. In Chelsea's senior year of high school, she was able to travel to London for an educational summer program offered by the local college. This allowed her to experience a bit of Europe, and I was so happy for her. Nicole was the creative one and was pursuing an Art degree. Whitney was studying math and physics with an interest in computer engineering. Erica performed well with the drama department in high school but decided to go back to New Jersey for her senior year where she graduated, and then moved back to California to attend college and then training in massage therapy. Jaime was raising her son and working as a pharmacy technician, and then chose to go back to school to pursue her college degree in Communications. She was expecting her second child. I was so proud of all of them!

I loved working in Hawaii, and the people became my 'ohana (family), but I was always so happy to come home to Huntington Beach! I had decided to stay, and I applied for my California state medical license. I continued traveling to work in Hawaii for about ten days every month. I learned to surf in the waves of Honolulu. Back in California, I also began formal martial arts training (at the age of 49), and I really enjoyed it, moving through belt levels with my mind set on achieving my black belt. At first, it was difficult for me to practice techniques that were meant to hurt other people's bodies. Interestingly, I learned from my sensei that the ancient Eastern practice was for one to first study healing the body for many years and only then learn how to damage it. (It seemed I was right on track.) I was also going to the gym on a very regular basis (in both CA and HI), doing cardio-kickboxing workouts at home, and generally enjoying my life.

After a few years, I came to learn about a communications professor at the local college with whom three of my daughters had taken classes. Jaime was insistent that I had to meet her. She tried to tell me that this professor was just like me - that she was talking about all the same things that I talked about - and that I should take her class. Well, "all the things I was talking about" were spirituality, God, astrology, Tarot, Kabbalah and magick.

I highly doubted that any of this was being discussed in a college class. I expressed my doubts to Jaime, but she persisted in her assertion. I was so glad that she was enjoying her teacher, and her classes, but I dismissed the notion that this professor was really getting into these topics, or that I would be interested in taking one of her classes. Finally, exasperated at my placating dismissals, Jaime put her class syllabus in front of me and starting to turn the pages so I could see what she had been talking about. I was shocked. Here was a college class that was teaching about auras and chakras and meditation and other spiritually aligned topics. Wow! California really was different!

I registered for this professor's class in the spring semester. Since I wasn't yet working in California, I could take this one afternoon class twice a week without missing too many of them. When I showed up on the first day of class, I introduced myself to this professor, Barbara, identifying myself as the mother of some of her students. We immediately connected and have been very close friends ever since! She is also a mother and had been studying spiritual topics for many years. As it turns out, she really was "just like me", as my daughter had tried to tell me.

During the course of the semester, Barbara invited many guest speakers to the class, and one of them presented information about the Modern Mystery School. I learned about something called a life activation, and also about an "initiation" class called Empower Thyself. It sounded interesting, but I wasn't really sure if it was any different from so many other spiritual programs that didn't appeal to me. I wasn't clear whether it had anything to offer me. Well, Barbara mentioned that I should have a life activation. It was described as a DNA activation that would "activate" my potential. I still didn't feel that I knew what it was, but it sounded like something good, and most importantly, I trusted her. She told me that her daughter, Theresa, offered the activation and that I could arrange the session directly with her. So, I dd.

When I showed up for my session, I had no idea what to expect. I followed Theresa's instructions, but I really didn't have to do anything. I sat in meditation for most of the session and was having some pretty cool images and sensations, but that wasn't entirely unusual for me. I also felt very calm, and I generally thought the whole experience was pretty unique.

When the session was over, I had some questions for Theresa about the initiation class, called Empower Thyself. Essentially, what I asked her was, "I'm doing pretty good where I'm at. How can this program help me?". I was not at all willing to jump into a weekend class if I didn't feel it was going to be worthy of my time and money. I did like that Theresa was a scientist like me and was similarly committed to spirituality. She answered my questions in a way that led me to think, "Maybe there's something here that can take me to my next level of understanding.", and I decided to check it out. So, I placed my deposit and marked my calendar for a couple months later.

I attended the class in the living room of a small apartment in Venice Beach with a couple other people. During the class, I was hearing a lot of information that was all very familiar to me and I felt comfortable. There were also concepts being presented that I hadn't heard before. That felt a little weird, but that's what I was there for – to hear things I hadn't heard before. Theresa explained that we didn't have to accept what was being presented as fact or reality. So, I didn't, but I did let it integrate over the following months, carefully pondering and considering all that I had heard.

At the end of the class weekend, the initiation ceremony was pretty magickal. It was simple, but it felt significant. Because Theresa had performed my initiation, she was called my Guide. I wasn't really sure what it was all about, but I trusted what I felt. And it all felt good. I was glad I had done the class. And there was more that I could do. I attended a few more small classes that were offered locally. Each time, I felt I was gaining something. I was slowly building an actual spiritual practice that I hadn't realized was missing from my life. Yes, I had a deep spiritual understanding and a strong connection to God, but no solid practice to anchor it all into my day-to-day life. It was also becoming apparent to me, over the months following initiation, that my spiritual progression had noticeably accelerated, more than I previously would have thought possible.

While I didn't dive full-bodied into this pool called the Modern Mystery School, I did keep going back to dip my feet in, gradually and tentatively wading just a little deeper to explore what they had to offer me. I still wasn't sure if this school was really worth my time and energy enough to "dive in". Spirituality was a priority for me, but I was very busy in my life, and I already felt pretty good about my spiritual progression. But I did need to know if this path might possibly hold that "something more" that I was looking for. I needed to find out.

In the meantime, I explored work in California while I waited for my state license to finalize. I knew there was a very nice hospital right on the coast, on the Pacific Coast Highway, that was just a few minutes from my house. I imagined how lovely it would be to work there! But I didn't even know if they had a NICU. As I explored this possibility, I discovered that they *did* have a NICU, and it offered the higher level of care that I preferred. But I had no idea how to find out if they were hiring or even who to contact. So, one day, I drove to the hospital, took the elevator to the NICU, and asked to speak with the director. He wasn't there, but I was able to speak with the neonatologist who was working that day. I learned that it was linked with a major southern California children's hospital, and that I could contact them about potential employment.

It wasn't long before I was hired and placed into a neonatologist position at that hospital. As soon as my state license went through, I began working there. I absolutely loved it! My partners, the nurses and all the staff were a joy to work with and I developed lasting friendships. The work, of course was stressful, the hours were long, and my life of chronic sleep deprivation continued, but I was doing everything I loved! My drive to work (and home) was an easy seven minutes down the Pacific Coast Highway. At the hospital, we had a beautiful view of the Pacific Ocean and southern California coastline. It was like a dream come true for me!

In addition to my "full-time" contracted hours in California, I continued to work my salaried position in Hawaii every month. This was possible because of how our schedules were arranged, and because I had the encouragement and support of my partners – in both Hawaii and California. Also, the Hawaiian hospital was so busy and the doctors there were so over-extended, that I just couldn't leave them with an open spot in their physician schedule. I knew how hard it was for them to hire doctors from the mainland to work on the island. And I enjoyed the contribution I was able to make, not just for the staff, but for those beautiful families.

We were still living in my rental house, and I knew it was time to buy again. I had made my decision to stay in Huntington Beach, so I began looking for a new house. I was already close to the beach, but I wanted to be closer! After months of looking at houses (I'm very particular about what I want), and with the help of a very experienced and very patient realtor, I found my house. It had everything I was looking for and was closer to the beach.

We moved into our new house just about six months after my initiation class. In that same timeframe, through the Modern Mystery School community in southern California, I had been invited to join an organized tour group traveling to Egypt. Now, I had always dreamt about traveling to Egypt! But what a big decision: Rearranging my work schedule, arranging the funds, flying halfway around the world to a new country that was in a state of unrest. But none of that seemed to matter to me very much. Very quickly, I made the decision to go! Even at the time, I was very aware that I probably would not have opened myself to that opportunity, and taken that action, if it wasn't for the life activation and initiation that I had received a few months prior. Days after we moved into our new house, I left for Egypt.

It really was the trip of a lifetime! We visited the Giza plateau and were able to do our own private ceremony in the King's chamber of the great pyramid. We hiked, first on camelback and then on foot, to sit at the top of Mt. Sinai on 11/11/11. We had a beautiful Nile cruise, and so much more! To this day, I am so thankful that I went on that trip. (I won't tell you about the Egyptian man I fell in love with. "A woman's heart is a deep ocean of secrets." [wink])

Looking back, I realized that in just a few months after my initiation, two major life events occurred: I purchased a southern California home of my own (that I continue to enjoy to this day), and I experienced a remarkable, once-in-a-lifetime guided tour through Egypt.

In the years following, I was taking more classes with the Mystery School and finding more benefit. My mind and my spiritual understanding were continuing to expand, and I was able to contemplate new things that allowed me to progress in my life. I was gradually receiving more activations and healing sessions because it felt like they were helping me to move forward in my spiritual progression. Consequently, my experience of my day-to-day life was significantly enhanced.

Honestly, I couldn't really explain how or why that was, but I had a clear sense that this Mystery School path was helping me get where I wanted to go. And there *was* a path I could follow, a structure for moving forward. Being a goal-oriented person, I liked that. It wasn't just a path of classes; it was a path of empowering tools and initiations. So, I was exploring higher levels of initiation and finding more and more personal fulfillment in my life. Everything was making even more sense than it did before. Additionally, I found myself in a position to be of service to others in yet another way.

Throughout my childhood, I was raised to be in service to others. My mother was always in service to the family and the household. I was taught to do the same and I emulated her. When we had house guests, my father taught me to tend to their needs and help them to feel at home and enjoy themselves. When I was twelve, I began doing work for my grandparent's business on the beach in the summers. We rented out large beach umbrellas (heavy wood and canvas) which we carried and set up for the customers, using a heavy iron spike to prepare a hole in the sand, and then we collected them in the evening. We also rented big, canvas rafts for use in the ocean, which had to sometimes be collected from the water.

My grandparents, and my entire extended Italian family, all had retail businesses of many different varieties in this New Jersey beach town where my mother had been raised: stores, a movie theater, a bar, restaurants, beach service, etc. I and my cousins all participated in one way or another "serving" people. We learned to be kind to all people, to treat them with respect and to help them in their needs. It was a way of life that has always served me very well in every area of my life. Whether this has been your experience or not, I can tell you that, for me, it has always been very fulfilling (even if it wasn't always easy) to be of service to other people.

So when I learned through the Mystery School that there were ways to be in service to others, it wasn't the idea of service that caused me to cringe. I understood service. In fact, I was in service all the time! I served my patients and their families to an extreme level of physical, mental, and emotional exertion, I served my family and my household. I was even traveling to Zimbabwe, Africa, volunteering with a medical charity. More service?! No thank you.

However, in that same memorable class where the idea of service was discussed, it was explained that the path of progression – the initiatory path – held multiple branches for being a Healer, a Teacher, and/or a Warrior. I remember talking to Theresa, my Guide, after the class and saying to her, with some deep recognition, "I am a healer, and a teacher, and a warrior.". She just looked at me and said, "Yes, you are.". I was beginning to see my purpose in the world from a higher, and a little deeper, perspective.

In future teaching and training with the Mystery School, I was learning that the most important service we can do is service to

97

the self - that it is only from a full cup that we can then truly serve others - from our overflow. Overflow? I was running on empty. But I was gradually learning to know myself on deeper and deeper levels that allowed me to then make shifts and changes, over time, that supported my physical and spiritual progression in life. Understanding service to self has been a big lesson for me.

I learned how important it is for us to not only serve ourselves, but to reconnect with the child that we all have within us. The little girl or boy who once found wonder and joy in life. What did we love to do way back then? Part of serving ourselves is getting back in touch with that.

It was two years after my first initiation that I attended what's called the Healers Academy. It was there that I was trained, among other things, to perform the life activation for others. I was beginning to see and understand the idea of service on a much higher level. I went on to do the life activation session for many people, and I watched as they received the benefits in their lives.

But quite honestly, I still was really just moving forward on this Mystery School path until I reached that place where I realized there was nothing more for me to gain – until it was no longer worth my time and energy. But that time never came.

At some point I realized that it was all there for me. I didn't need to look anywhere else. It was just a question of how far I wanted to go. Well, I kept going and my life kept becoming more fulfilling. I was also able be in service to others on another level, supporting them in their own spiritual progression, which I really loved and valued. It brought me a sense of joy, greater than I had known in service before. I was still working as a neonatologist. I still felt, every day, that doing that work was exactly where I belonged in the world. And it was! But I was beginning to see that there could be <u>more</u>. My idea of how I could serve my purpose in the world was expanding. My service to others in their spiritual progression was bringing more joy into my life! And because I had learned the importance of serving myself first, I was able to do just that.

I was doing the work of a life activation practitioner, and I had become a teacher, and then eventually a Guide, within the Modern Mystery School. I was also doing the work I had always loved in a NICU seven minutes from my house. Physical fitness remained an important part of my life, including body building, kickboxing, hiking, and martial arts training. My daughters were enjoying the freedom to make of their lives what they wanted, and they were happy. I had a very healthy (albeit still chronically sleep-deprived) life, and I was happy.

In my younger years, I had always fancifully planned to retire at the age of 50. That didn't happen, but I was in my 50's, and I was formulating a plan to wean myself out of the chronic stress of neonatology and into full-time Mystery School work. Life was good.

I had found a path for my spiritual progression that, to some extent, I had been looking for. But in my searching, I never fully believed that such a complete, structured program existed, or that it was possible to find - even while I was beginning to study and train within it! I can now see why. There is nothing else in our "matrix" world for us to compare it to. Our minds have no point of reference for understanding it, or what it offers. In fact, it isn't really _of_ this world; it did not originate with human thought or the human mind.

Because we humans are so much more than just physical beings, what we require to move toward truly Knowing Thyself must come from beyond the physical matrix world, because our true essence is the life of eternal spirit. That is why so many of us find connection, solace, and fulfillment in our relationship with God, whatever that may be. It feels like home. It is home. And it gives us a peek into finding ourselves. However, we tend to still have more questions and seek more fulfillment. Often, we feel a need for something more.

As I walked this Mystery School path, there were many times I heard the question in my mind, "What am I doing?!". Walking this path was so "out of the box", it was natural to ask myself this question. In those moments, when my mind didn't have an answer, I would always find myself back in my heart where it felt good. And it felt right. Trusting my intuition had always served me well in my life. So, I went with it. In so doing, I was moving my mind out of the matrix world. I had taken the red pill, so to speak. My perspective of life, and _my_ life, was now coming from a higher understanding, beyond the mediocrity of the matrix.

I have now referenced "the matrix" several times, and it is an analogy to the movie, The Matrix. In the movie, Neo, the hero, is given a choice, an opportunity to take a red pill that would allow him to discover more about what the world looks like from behind the scenes – the *real* world without the illusions that we think are real, or a blue pill that allows him to stay in his life as he knows it. He takes the red pill, finds himself behind the scenes – in the real world without illusion, and learns that the world's situation is actually dire. He is told that he is "The One" who can save the world, which he doesn't believe. Eventually (spoiler alert) he comes to find that he is "The One". In my analogy, the idea of the "matrix world" is a way to view reality, the way most people view it, and it can then be an analogy to move beyond it. But in this version, we can <u>all</u> be The One!

Over years of study and training, I realized that, because of this path, I had attained a place of real fulfillment within myself – a sense of alignment between myself in this life and the highest essence of myself, beyond the matrix. Now please understand, in the days before my life activation, I would have told you that I already had that. At that time, I was very much at peace within myself and with my spiritual knowledge, from my own study as well as my own direct experiences. But here was a BIG lesson for me. THERE CAN ALWAYS BE MORE! There can always be more to your purpose, to who you are and what you do in this world. You can always enjoy life more!

But do you <u>want</u> more? Some of us do, and some of us don't. That's OK. We all get to choose our own path in life.

At this place in *my* life, I was pretty comfortable. Still, I've always been one of those people who wanted more. Little did I know what was coming next...

Conjunction

In the fourth stage of Alchemy, Conjunction, there is a reuniting within the self, a rectification that follows all the previous work. This unification within allows us to find the empowerment of our true selves, which often brings increased intuitive insight. It is an evolution of the spiritual self in its search for perfection. We could say it is a place where we begin to find our way home, our way to our connection with God.

Conjunction brings us to a place of harmonization within. We feel more confident in knowing who we are, of our own divinity and our connection with that. It feels good. From here we can continue to move forward (as long as we don't get too comfortable).

My Experience:

Even though I felt complete, in a sense, with my spiritual understanding and my life in general, at the time I moved to

California, I knew that there was more to learn, and I was still searching. I was very discerning about where I might find that, but I remained open to the possibility of finding a deeper understanding. In so doing, I found a true spiritual path of progression, that in the years prior, I wasn't sure even existed. I had brought myself home.

I learned the importance of serving myself, filling my own cup first, so I could serve others even more, and that serving my own spiritual progression allowed the cup from which I was serving to be even bigger. I also learned that serving others in *their* spiritual progression brought greater joy than any other service I had done.

I felt fulfilled in my life as a neonatologist, knowing that I was living my purpose in the world, but I learned that there can always be more!

My Guidance:

Remain discerning, but don't close your mind to finding a deeper understanding of who you are. To Know Thyself is a lifelong endeavor – and beyond. In that vein, I encourage you to explore what the Modern Mystery School has to offer that might support you. You're never so good that you can't learn something more (about yourself).

Serve yourself first. Be kind and loving toward yourself. Take the trip, enjoy the good china, buy the nice shoes. Look for where you might be depriving yourself, sacrificing your own well-being, or operating from a place of imbalance in your service, and seek to rectify that. Make sure you are taking the time to do some of the things that brought you joy as a child.

If your answer to my question, "Do you <u>want</u> more?" was, "No, I can't handle more. I'm good.", but the child within you isn't happy, or you feel this answer is coming from a sense of just settling, or exhaustion, I recommend seeking an activation and/or healing session with a Mystery School practitioner. It will help you to have more clarity about the choices you're making in your life. (By the way, so will connecting with your inner child. That could be your first step in sorting out what you really want in life.)

[<u>Benefits of the life activation include</u>: more clarity regarding who you are and your unique potential, infusion of Light (positive energy) into physical body, awakening of dormant talents and abilities, more emotional stability, relief from anxiety and stress.]

Carla's Pearls

"What if...?"

"I matter. Taking care of myself matters!"

"There can always be more."

SONG

"CABARET" – Liza Minelli

https://www.youtube.com/watch?v=5QS1l1mSDSo

What Did You Learn About Yourself from This Chapter?

[Write about it here]

PART THREE:
EMBRACING LIFE

CHAPTER 5

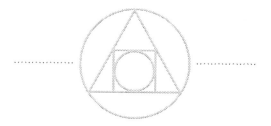

The Alchemy of Being Brought to Your Knees:

Chronic Illness

Fermentation

(Rising above)

In this chapter, you will discover deep insight into how to find your way through unforeseen physical challenges and rise above it.

Yes, I was one of those people who says, "I want more.". I guess I've *always* been that kind of person. (If you've read my story so far, you're probably saying, "Uh, yeah.")

I was very happy with how I had been orchestrating my life to this point. I was asking for more and I was getting more. So far, so good. But my life's greatest challenge was growing beneath the surface, unable to be seen. It was all very insidious. I had no idea where my life was about to take me, and I would have *never* believed it.

As I am beginning to write this chapter, I am feeling a sense of sadness. It is coming from a memory of the grief that came with watching my life disintegrate, what I thought was my *whole* life, and then finding the transformation into a new life. A new life that I would have never chosen, but that would allow me to recreate myself and to discover a far greater connection to my true essence than ever before.

In the Mystery School lineage, we recognize:

"You are an eternal being. You have never been born. Therefore, you can never die."

Gudni GED Gudnason

Founder of the Modern Mystery School

Head Ipsissimus in the Lineage of King Salomon

I had thought I understood this but remember what we learned in the previous chapter: There can always be more. Now, my understanding of this statement was being brought to a whole new level.

As I said, it began insidiously. I started to forget things. In the beginning, my daughters and I would laugh about it. For example, there was the time I couldn't find any of the Christmas presents I had bought for one of my daughters. (I could've sworn they were all in one pile, somewhere in the garage, but I couldn't find them.) So, I went out and bought a whole new collection of gifts for her. (Eventually, I found the first set of gifts.)

"How could you buy a whole bunch of Christmas presents and forget you bought them, and then buy a whole different set?!"

"I thought I just dreamed that I bought them."

We all knew I was always sleep deprived, so we just laughed. Mom is so silly!

My capacity for physical training and for reaching fitness goals was very slowly deteriorating. "Maybe I'm just having a bad day. Maybe I didn't get enough sleep." I still had good days, but the frequency of the "not so good" days was beginning to increase. Then I began to notice that I could no longer modulate my lean body mass and body fat; everything that I knew, everything that used to work was no longer working. It was like I was living in some parallel universe. "Maybe I'm just getting old." But yet, the basics of regulating my diet and exercise regime for controlling my physical body should have still applied, even if on a different level. I pushed myself harder and harder, doing what had always worked, but I kept gaining weight - and losing fitness capacity. Nothing made any sense.

And then there was the fatigue. Well, of course I was tired! I was chronically sleep deprived, doing work that was stressful on every level of my being, and even though I had found some semblance of balance, I still loved to push myself to enjoy life even more! (That was one of the reasons I loved being physically fit. I could DO so much more! - skiing, hiking, surfing, literally climbing mountains, and really engaging with life!) I had already been diagnosed with an underactive thyroid. So, I had my medication dose increased, but nothing changed. I figured I was just getting older and therefore I just couldn't do as much. I had wanted to gradually make the transition out of the hospital to doing more Mystery School work anyway. So, I reduced my hours at the hospital from a full-time schedule to part-time. Also, I decided to give up my position in Hawaii, after nearly ten years. Now I would be able to have a schedule that was more conducive to rest and relaxation. I would be able to get more sleep. Surely that would help. It made good, logical sense.

However, being a doctor with an acute understanding of the body's physiology, as well as being very experienced with training my own body to a high level of athleticism for many years, I remained perplexed. Something was wrong. I sought advice from a wide multitude of healthcare practitioners, including medical doctors, and ultimately, I found no help. First, it was my thyroid, then it was my adrenals, then, no, it really was my thyroid. My chi flow was decreased in certain meridian channels and acupuncture should help; it did for short periods of time. Then, the medical specialist for metabolism confirmed, "Nope. It's not your thyroid.". I was also receiving various forms of energy healing. I pursued the appropriate blood tests, treatment, and follow up for everyone's diagnostic assessment, medical and alternative, but absolutely nothing was helping. In fact, everything was getting worse.

I was still going to the gym, but again, my workouts seemed to be having no effect at all on my state of health or well-being. I had always balanced my workouts with my own form of yoga practice and chi exercises, and I continued with this. Yet and still, my fitness level continued to fall. My recovery time from a physical workout could last for days – days of being able to do next to nothing. But I continued to do what had always worked. I pushed myself.

Through these years, I had headaches almost every morning; I even vomited once or twice for no apparent reason. My vision seemed to be getting worse by the week. I was losing my ability to regulate my body temperature – sometimes I was overheated and sometimes I was really cold. I had muscle cramping. There were times I was dizzy and light-headed. (Back when I was still working in Hawaii, I actually had a bout of vertigo for several weeks – something I had never had before.) I had intermittent times of confusion and disorientation, and my memory loss was getting worse, for both past and recent memories. It was difficult to maintain my mental focus or a process of thought. And my nervous system was becoming overly sensitive – to light and sound, and just about any stimulus.

But more than anything, it was the fatigue that became horribly debilitating. I would need to lie down, more and more often, even after certain minimal degrees of effort, whether mental or physical, that had never created that need before. I began to notice that *whenever* I would lie down, I had overwhelming shortness of breath accompanied by uncontrolled shaking of my arms. I had a pulmonary (lung) and cardiology (heart) evaluations and again, all was normal; nothing was wrong. Yes. Something is very wrong. My next specialist was going to be a neurologist.

After this progressive decline over about four years, my life was reduced to a bare minimum of activity. It was simply some alternation of going to my (reduced) work at the hospital (for my usual 24-hour shifts), going to the gym and lying on the sofa. That was all I could do. Even at work, whenever my presence was not acutely needed, I was lying down, with the lights off – short of breath and shaking. I was literally living in darkness.

Finally, the light came in. (Even if, initially, it didn't seem like it.)

My kitchen sink – yes, my kitchen sink, stay with me. My kitchen sink would occasionally, over the years, seem to be causing water to leak onto the kitchen floor from under the cabinet, creating small puddles near the area where the sink and dishwasher were situated. Sometimes it would seem to happen when the dishwasher was running and sometimes not. Sometimes it was related to a sink clog and sometimes not. But the sink would randomly "clog" and that always created a water leak on the floor. Plumbers would come, relieve the clog, and convince me that it was all very normal and not unusual. I was told that all of our water leaks over the previous few years were simply attributed to "sink clogging".

On one (final) occasion, water began leaking profusely onto the floor, from under the cabinets, and it was a huge leak that wasn't stopping. I again called the plumber - same company but a new guy showed up. He explored the reason for the leak with diligence and persistence. (Light coming in.) He determined that the source of the leak had to be coming from behind the wall, and he asked my permission to knock a small hole in the wall, through the back of the cabinet under the sink. I said, "Yes, please!". (I could tell he was the one that could figure this out.)

Long story short, he found the source of the leak. It was from a sewage drainpipe behind the wall of the kitchen; it had ruptured. It had probably been slowly leaking over the years, creating intermittent flooding, until it finally ruptured. The plumber told me that when he broke through the wall, he saw a lot of dark mold growth and was unable to explore any further. Protocol required that he call in a remediation specialist. He did and I thanked him for all he had done to help me.

I didn't really know what a remediation team did, but they

came the next day. I was surprised to see them donning suits and masks like it was some kind of toxic quarantine, and I didn't understand why. They said they would be clearing out all the mold from my kitchen. I was thinking, "It's just mold. We had it in every basement in the northeast. What's the big deal?". But I didn't say anything to them. I let them do their job. They told me that there was an incredibly large amount of mold, black mold, and many other varieties, mixed with varieties of bacteria, growing throughout my kitchen, behind the cabinets and in the hidden walls. Apparently, it was very impressive, even to them. It had been there for a long time, growing and expanding, and I had no idea. My entire kitchen and part of the dining room was taken down to studs.

Meanwhile, my curiosity about why everybody was making so much fuss over mold led me to search about it online. Very quickly, I discovered that certain molds can be toxic and create health issues for some people. (I vaguely remembered this from my medical training, but it was such an obscure area that was relegated to adult infectious disease – not my realm.) As I delved deeper, some of the symptoms described were memory loss, fatigue, shortness of breath, nervous system impairment...wait, what?! Every single unexplained symptom that I had was on the checklist. In fact, I was able to check off all the boxes! Prior to this revelation of mine, my symptoms had all seemed completely unrelated to each other; I had no idea how to fit them all into one cause. And obviously, neither did any of the many healthcare practitioners I had seen.

It looked like there was a way to diagnose this condition and even treat it! I swiftly moved my search to find a practitioner who was trained to do this. It sure seemed like this long-term mold exposure was the reason for what was happening to me, but I wanted to be sure. It was all new to me. And then, if it was, I wanted to find out what I could do about it. There were only a dozen or so specialized practitioners across the country, but I found a qualified medical doctor who was just an hour drive from my house! I called and made an appointment.

During my first visit with this doctor, I was impressed. My nature is to be objectively critical and also intuitive. As an experienced intensive care physician as well, I was paying close attention – as much as I could in my physical and mental state at the time. He took plenty of time with me. He was checking all my boxes for what constitutes a knowledgeable, competent, compassionate, and communicative doctor. I could trust him.

After a thorough physical examination, an MRI of my brain and a lot of blood tests, it was clear. I had what was called CIRS – chronic inflammatory response syndrome – from a toxic mold exposure. I was familiar with SIRS – an acute systemic inflammatory response syndrome – that could result from life threatening bacterial infections or trauma, but I had never heard of this.

He explained that I had some chronic brain swelling and other brain changes that were causing my neurologic symptoms. And there were a whole host of metabolic derangements in my body that were also part of this process and that explained all of my physical and mental deterioration for the past several years, including the weight gain. Next question: Can I get better? The answer was yes. In fact, I was told that the probability was pretty good. I was so encouraged! I just needed to follow the treatment protocol. And give it time.

I was so relieved to just know that there was an explanation for everything that was happening to me! There was a name for it! I had a diagnosis! And there was a treatment plan with a good chance of recovery. I was told that I could probably recover 80-90% of my previous functioning. My attitude was, "Well, if that's what the average is, surely I will recover 100%.". I knew that before I got sick, I was exceedingly healthy; I had a strong will and discipline to do things in my life that most people didn't do, and I had all my spiritual tools and training to support me. I was very hopeful.

I spent time learning as much as I could about this condition. There was quite a bit of published scientific and clinical research that had been done, but it was all fairly recent, within the previous ten years or so. The medical community at large had absolutely no training or education about it, except for the few specialists who had chosen to study with the physician who first described it. I certainly had never heard about it, or anything like it. (I wish I had.) But that explained why no one I had sought care from before had any understanding of it.

In the month or so following my diagnosis, even though I had only been working part-time, it became clear that I could no longer work at all. At the hospital, my partners knew that I had been struggling with unexplained fatigue, but I had never let it interfere with my level of care for the babies and their families. I always pushed myself to do whatever needed to be done - and then I crashed in my own time. But now, I couldn't even remember the patients' information between one incubator and the next.

Throughout my career as a neonatologist, I could always be depended upon for my memory of details as well as accuracy in my patient care and communication, but it was all disintegrating. One of my partners suggested that maybe I needed to take some time off. (By the way, intensivist doctors will hardly ever say that; most will work until they drop, and some actually do.) So, with an actual diagnosis, I took a short-term disability leave, fully expecting to get better. I stopped going to the gym since it wasn't helping and seemed to be making things worse. Now I could rest all the time, as much as I needed.

In the ensuing months, I followed the treatment protocol, had my blood tested frequently and followed up with the doctor often. He continued to be incredibly supportive. But I was not getting better. I knew it was going to take time, but I was now essentially bed ridden. No amount of sleep or rest was helping. In fact, ironically, I had difficulty sleeping (which is a recognized part of this condition).

Even though the light had come in, and I had a diagnosis and a treatment plan, I was still very much in a dark place.

My short-term leave became a long-term leave. I couldn't

do much of anything. I wanted to believe that the treatment plan was working, but I still could not function. I was seeing some improvement, but I still had severe fatigue, shortness of breath, and weakness. I was having wild swings in temperature regulation. Often after eating (it didn't matter what it was or how much), I would be overheated and sweating (worse than the hot flashes of menopause) and hardly able to catch my breath or even keep my eyes open. Then I would be so cold that nothing could help me get warm.

The episodes of dizziness, confusion, and disorientation were happening less often, but still occurred. Visual tracking remained very difficult for me, and so reading, which I had always loved, was infrequent and very limited. The generalized shaking whenever I would lie down was getting much better, but now I was developing more focal tremors that had become localized to my right hand and left foot. My memory was gradually getting better as was my ability to focus and process, but these functions remained significantly impaired. I also still had nervous system sensitivity, including to light and sound, but it was better than before.

Once the formal treatment protocol was completed and it was clear that I wasn't "better", I began to seek more alternative treatments. I wasn't giving up. I discovered, along with my doctor, that my temperature instability, and probably some of my fatigue and shortness of breath, and my racing heart rate, were due to an exaggerated histamine response in my body. There were treatments for that, and they were helping, but they didn't resolve these issues.

I tried every alternative therapy I could find that seemed to have some potential for helping me. Some didn't help at all. Others were promising for a while, but ultimately weren't making any difference. I continued to receive many energy healing sessions as well. By this time, I had exhausted the time frame for my long-term disability leave from the hospital. My employer had chosen to hold my position for me even beyond that time frame, despite the financial burden to the group, but it had just been too long. Unfortunately, I had to retire. I couldn't ask them to continue to hold my position, especially since I had no idea if I would ever be able to work again. I was physically and mentally unable to perform the duties of a neonatologist – or even an average human.

Essentially, I was moving into a more chronic state of illness, and that's where I have stayed. Over these past several years, immunosuppressants helped me to some extent when precious little did, but they have side effects that aren't desirable – especially during a global pandemic. I have continued to explore any and all potential therapies, diets and supplements that may benefit me to find what helps.

Speaking of my diet, a few years ago I started eating just twice a day, going 16-20 hours without eating, almost every day. This has been good for me for several reasons. All my symptoms get worse anytime I eat, no matter what it is, so not eating is good. And, intermittent fasting, of which this is a variation, is supposed to have some health benefits. Also, my caloric intake has to remain low; if I eat much more than a basal metabolic rate worth of calories, I consistently gain weight. Losing weight has not been possible, at least not yet.

I still experience extreme fatigue, muscle weakness, shortness of breath, and exhaustion. The funny thing is, my whole life, I was "used to" being tired. I dealt with it. I got rest when I could, and I learned to live with it. And the more healthy, fit, and active I was in general, the easier it was to tolerate. But this fatigue has been completely different! This kind of exhaustion is nothing I could have ever been able to fathom without having experienced it, even with my 30 years of sleep deprivation.

I still have mild tremors of my right hand and left foot, occasional confusion, and continued memory challenges. I still have neuro-sensitivity, but I have adapted to it. I have hired people to help me with many of the things I can no longer do. I wear sunglasses whenever necessary, and I use noise-modifying ear buds when needed. When my body reacts to sudden noises or vibrations, I can usually bring myself back to stillness. It is just my physical body and my brain; it is not my mind. I can control my mind.

I have good days and bad days. Sometimes I feel well, and sometimes I feel so unwell that I just cry. The energy available for my physical body to function flows at a trickle and comes at a premium. At baseline, I have shortness of breath with any exertion and my heart races. This includes things like making my bed in the

123

morning, brushing my hair, carrying one light bag of groceries, or getting a quick shower; washing my hair is a whole different level of exertion. It used to be very difficult for me to walk up a flight of stairs, but that is somewhat better now. I just have to go slow. In fact, everything I do, I have to do slowly. What a huge shift in lifestyle this has been for me!

I can almost always push myself to do things, if I choose, but I have to pay for that later, sometimes needing a full day of recovery time, and sometimes requiring much longer than that, to get back to "baseline". And whenever my body is overextended, I find that my mental function deteriorates in tandem. Nevertheless, I have found a state of equipoise with all of this. I have learned how to regulate my activity and my level of exertion. I know what I can handle and what is out of balance – for me. I can choose when it's important to me to overextend myself, and then plan for my recovery. I have come to know myself on a whole new level. (More on that in a little bit.)

My current diagnosis is best depicted as CFS/ME (chronic fatigue syndrome/myalgic encephalomyelitis) and CIRS (chronic inflammatory response syndrome). My doctor tells me that even among his many patients with CIRS, I am among the most extremely affected. Lucky me! (I knew I was special.) There are definitely certain genetic patterns that can make someone more susceptible to develop, and be chronically affected by, this condition.

Many people can be exposed to toxic forms of mold and seemingly be completely unaffected. Many people can be affected with memory loss and severe fatigue due to the mold in their environment, but once they are removed from that environment, they recover completely. Others do not, but then they can respond well to treatment. (And incidentally, now we have something in the world called "long haul Covid". It has many similarities and overlaps with ME/CFS and CIRS, and is drawing the attention of science and medicine, which brings opportunity for more light to come in.)

Perhaps my situation is some combination of my genetics and my repeated, chronic mold exposures over the course of my life, and then the extreme and long-term exposure in my kitchen, that brought my body to some "point of no return". Maybe pushing my physical training, when I didn't know what was happening to my body, created some "point of no return". Who knows? We still have so much to learn about this particular constellation of dis-ease of the physical body. But I have come a long way.

With all that I have learned about my body, and with various treatments, both ancient and modern, and lifestyle adaptations, I have a fairly viable life now. I am able to enjoy more physical functionality than before, even though it is still quite limited. I no longer feel like I am dying every day. I have more life in my body, and I am so grateful for that!

However, this was a place that I would have never, in a million years, *ever* thought would be my experience. I always took care of my body and my overall health. I wasn't fanatical (OK, maybe I was close). I was raised with the example of physical health and well-being, and I had always been supported in that for myself. How in the world could I be "chronically ill"?! Wasn't that something that happened to people who didn't take care of themselves?

I was having a real shift in how I viewed this idea of chronic illness. Of course, I understood that cancers and genetic disorders and traumas and various other circumstances put people in situations where they had some degree of chronic illness. But now, I was having my own direct experience with it. I was having to negotiate and reconcile with it in my own day-to-day life. In the past, I had some understanding, and compassion, but now I had real empathy and a far greater understanding.

I remember back when I worked in Philadelphia in the 1990's, one of the nurses shared with me that she was having severe fatigue. She didn't understand why it was happening, and nothing was helping her; she was expressing her quiet desperation to me. She was a hard-working nurse and a very good human. She loved her work in the NICU but ended up having to leave it. At that time, chronic fatigue syndrome (CFS), as a condition, was just barely beginning to be recognized as something real. I remember feeling and expressing compassion for her, but I had no reference point for understanding what she was going through. I wanted to be able to help her, but I had nothing.

With this new evolution in my perspective of chronic fatigue and chronic illness coming from my own direct experience and coupled with my now years of training in the mystery school, I was beginning to move into greater wisdom about my life and life in general. Furthermore, and perhaps more importantly, my compassion for myself and for others, which had always been strong, was now expanding – a lot.

In my training in the Mystery School, I had learned that holding onto mental or emotional attachments consumes so much of our energy, energy that we could be using for other things. Over the years, I began to understand this concept on deeper and deeper levels, learning how to just "let go" and not waste my energy. Then, I found myself in a situation where I literally had NO energy. Well guess what? Whatever mental or emotional attachments I was still holding onto, I was very aware of them and the energy they were taking. I could not allow even the slightest drain on my energy. I had to just let them go. None of it mattered anymore.

What about building and replenishing energy in the body? Many spiritual practices work with what can be called Chi, the life force energy that flows through our body. We can access our Chi through our breath, and there are many techniques for doing this. Learning to work with Chi gives us the possibility of accessing infinite universal energy to flow through us. In the past, without even realizing it, it was my regular physical activity as well as my own variation of yoga and Chi work that allowed me to flow abundant Chi through my body. Ironically, I then found myself with very low Chi, and whatever I could build up would quickly dissipate.

I learned to focus on accessing Chi in much more subtler ways, without having to exert the precious energy of moving my physical body. I could get energy directly from the universe itself.

I have always loved the beach. But now, I was learning that this was more than just a place of enjoyment for me. I could find joy and actual rejuvenation from simply standing near the beach, breathing in the salt air, connecting with the flow and energy of the waves, the warmth of the sun's rays, and even from the sand through my feet. In fact, my connection with nature in all forms became enhanced, and my awareness heightened, because of my experience with such an extreme energy depletion. I can now view the Earth, and the whole universe, as a pure source of energy. I receive joy and love from watching the beauty of the sunrise through my bedroom window. I have learned to see the beauty of divinity everywhere and in everything. The pure and simple joys of being alive. I am alive!

I do maintain hope that I will one day be able to shift the process in my physical body so that I can once again maintain physical energy, and Chi that can flow at much higher levels. In the Mystery School lineage, we know that there is a new paradigm possible for healthcare. There are many ancient tools, as well as new cutting-edge technologies, that can allow us to move forward in our ability to heal – on all levels. I have experienced and greatly benefitted from both of these. For real healing, we need to address ALL of us. We need to use all that works, from the ancient tools to the new technology. I can see a time when, what we call miracles today, will be commonplace healing. But for now, as far as my physical situation goes, I have adapted. I have lived, I have progressed, and I have learned.

Even as my physical body, and my ability to engage with the world through the activity of my body, was deteriorating, I have always maintained my spiritual progression, moving forward on the path of spiritual progression. As you may be beginning to see, it has helped me tremendously! I began to see so many aspects of my situation from a higher perspective - a perspective of empowerment that comes from Knowing Thyself on deeper and deeper levels. I was in control. I was gradually finding a way to recreate my life and move forward in my life.

In doing so, I began to realize that I simply had a "new brain", and that's how I began to talk about it. Even though I had areas of my brain that were impaired, I wasn't a "victim" of brain injury. I wasn't someone who was "plagued" with a memory deficit or was in some situation I couldn't control. I began to view any mishaps of my brain with amusement. I was being entertained. It was a fun adventure. Whenever I found myself misspeaking, or getting confused, or forgetful, I would say to myself, or to others if present, "Oh, that's my new brain!", and we could laugh. Silly brain!

Over the years, I also had learned to tell myself, "I love you." I would often lay in bed and repeat "I love you" to myself, over and over and over. I did this nearly every morning and every night and many times in between. It was necessary. And it has helped a great deal! I also began reciting variations on a mantra: "It's OK. I'm doing good. I'm doing great. Life is good.". I still, to this day, find myself using this.

In my personal experience with chronic illness, I was able

to shift and transform myself and my life so much more because I was equipped with the tools and the empowerment of the Mystery School path, seeing myself more and more beyond my physical body. And then, in turn, my chronic illness experience was helping me to accelerate my spiritual progression! Spiritual progression accelerates life progression, and life progression accelerates spiritual progression. Ultimately, spiritual progression IS life progression!

Remember back in chapter three, talking about physical fitness, when I said that our physicality is so effective at supporting our spiritual progression? Well, I had now learned this on a much deeper level.

When aspects of our physical body functioning have become chronically incapable, it's easy to get stuck in the energy of "I'm not a capable person". But it's so important to know that our physical body is NOT who we are. I have a physical body, but… I am not my physical body. Our true essence is spirit! Spirit is the essence of life that animates our body. Corpses don't have that "life" because the spirit has left. I am an eternal, spirit being. And oh boy, life was giving me a crash course on taking that teaching to a much deeper level!

Now, even if you know, on any level, that your true essence is spirit, it does not alleviate the immense frustration and deep sadness that comes with having a body that no longer enables you to do the things you used to do, or to engage with the world the way you want to. There can be a deep depression and a time of wondering, "What's the point?". I completely understand that!

But you can move beyond that. We must *not* hold onto the mentality of being a victim. Sure, we may ask, "Why me?". But at some point, hopefully sooner rather than later, we must remind ourselves that life doesn't have to just *happen* to us. We <u>do</u> have control. We <u>do</u> have a choice. We will always find ourselves in many different unexpected life situations, but then, what can we do about it? There's always *something* we can do, no matter how trivial it may seem. Taking control in even the smallest way can open doors to taking control in bigger ways.

Along with the mentality of victimhood, if we hold onto that, comes the search for someone or something to blame. We might say, "Well it's certainly not my fault!". Alternatively, if you've studied any new age philosophy, you might be tempted to actually blame yourself (or the person who has been affected) for "creating it" through the energy of thoughts and/or emotions. Sure, these can contribute to illness, but so do so many things! Our world has so many toxins, diseases, accident potentials, and environmental mine fields - and there is mental illness, emotional illness, and spiritual illness. But none of this really matters! Is it your fault? Absolutely not. The point is that it isn't *anybody's* fault. What matters most is that we can use our power and take control from where we are *now*. We can take responsibility. We can figure out what we *can* do to make things better and do it.

What about, "It's not fair!". Remember what I told my

children? It doesn't have to be. Do you really want life to be fair? Do you want it to be easy? Or do you like being challenged and having those sweet victories? Do you want a world where nothing you do matters or has any consequence? Or would you prefer to have some power to control your own life and your own destiny? I personally love "the thrill of victory and the agony of defeat", as they say. This is life! Every time we feel "the agony of defeat" and then find a way to overcome it, we have victory! We can always create victory for ourselves. We can earn that sweetness. Would it be as sweet if it wasn't earned? The energy of "earning" brings us more power, more empowerment.

Whatever you're going through, it has absolutely nothing to do with fairness. I did everything in my power, my whole life, to maintain my physical and mental health and well-being. When I began to notice something was wrong, I searched everywhere for help – I'm even a doctor myself – but there were no answers. After my body continued to move into debilitation, and I finally found answers and a treatment plan, it didn't work. I didn't get better. But I have overcome the senselessness of it, the frustration, the grief, and the perceived limitations. It had nothing to do with victimhood, fault, blame or fairness. It had to do with having the awareness, tools, and power to know who I am, and act based on that knowledge and understanding. Heaven knows, I allowed myself moments of having a "pity party". But then we have to move on.

Let's look at another example regarding the idea of hardship and struggle in life. Babies in the womb require the resistance of the fluid that they're floating in, and of the uterine wall limitation that surrounds them; they require this resistance in order for their physical body to develop and form normally. Without this resistance, the body cannot form normally. They may not even be able to survive outside the womb. Even though we are no longer in the womb, we still require resistance to grow and to develop. However, now, it is up to us to decide, and to consciously provide that resistance for ourselves. So that we can learn and grow and move forward.

This is the Alchemy of hardship. Whenever we go through hardship or trauma in our life, and find a way to overcome it, that brings us a little more power and more understanding that we can use to keep moving us forward. It's another steppingstone for us to *be* more and *do* more. Furthermore, it is through service to other people that we grow even faster. If we choose to use these assets that we have funded for ourselves to then also help and serve others, we become wiser, we gain the power of wisdom. This is the cycle of Alchemy and transformation.

Sometimes, when we have struggles, we tend to look back with regret, at what we perceive as some kind of failure, and on some level, we identify with "being" a failure. Then, our mind will often use our perception of that experience to predict doom and failure in the future, and we believe it! We believe in a future that hasn't even happened yet. Please know that anything we have done in the past has absolutely *nothing* to do with our future! No matter where we are, we can choose to face forward, and move on from <u>there</u>. Focusing on the past, or the future, will never help us now.

We must always remember that everyone is struggling through something, and most of the time it cannot be seen. It's so important for us to find compassion for others. Believe it or not, finding compassion for others becomes much easier when we begin to have more compassion for ourselves. Always look for opportunities to show yourself more love and more compassion. Through my illness - by bringing brought to my knees - I was compelled to do this on a much deeper level. It's a good thing.

One final note. Life is not perfect. You can try to eat the best food, exercise, have a healthy environment, get good sleep, but life will disrupt it. Life is not meant to be perfect. It's about: How are you going to respond? How are you going to act NOW, that you didn't have enough sleep, that you can't exercise anymore, that you can't have the perfect diet, perfect environment, etc.? Imperfection is part of life. Do what you CAN do to make it as perfect as it can be. Find your bliss and enjoy it!

For me, Rocky, my Philadelphia hero, said it best:

"Let me tell you something you already know. The world ain't all sunshine and rainbows. It's a very mean and nasty place and I don't care how tough you are, it will beat you to your knees and keep you there permanently if you let it. You, me, or nobody is gonna hit as hard as life. But it ain't about how hard you hit. It's about how hard you can *get* hit and keep moving forward. That's how winning is done."

Remember, when you overcome *your* illness, *your* challenge, *your* obstacle, think about all the people that you will then be able to help get through the same thing - because *you* got through it. You'll have developed an understanding and from that understanding, you'll be able to help them.

There is no doubt in my mind, and maybe you have been able to see, that my alchemical transformation through my illness, to my new life and my "new brain", would barely have been possible without the awareness, tools, and power that came with walking the initiatory path of the mystery school — the path to Know Thyself. (Or, it would have taken me many years longer, maybe too long.) I also know that, throughout my life, my inner healing and transformation could only be done by one person - me. Moreover, as a result of my progression forward, I am able to continue being in service to others and doing the work that is so important to me — helping others. I now know that you don't have to be a doctor to save lives. We can all do that.

I had to go through the chaos of the unknown and the uncertain. Chaos is a necessary part of Alchemy and transformation, but having the tools to facilitate my navigation *through* the chaos was invaluable. Now, I feel like a phoenix that is rising from the ashes. I can say, more sincerely than ever before, I love my life!

But wait, there's more…

Fermentation

The fifth stage of Alchemy, Fermentation, occurs in two parts: descent into death and return to life. We are moving from having a connection to Spirit to bringing Spirit into our darkness to create new life. There is a fire in the soul. It is likened to the phoenix rising from the ashes. Alchemists have described this stage as "living inspiration from above".

Dennis William Hauck said in "The Emerald Tablet: Alchemy for Personal Transformation":

"Fermentation is the introduction of new life into the product of Conjunction to completely change its characteristics – that is, to completely raise it to a new level of being.

It's as if our consciousness has left the bounds of matter and exists outside our bodies, and everything we experience in this state is more real and more truthful than the everyday world."

According to Dr. Theresa Bullard in "The Game Changers: Social Alchemists in the 21st Century":

"It takes discipline, patience, and dedication...The only way to speed it up is through various initiatory and inner soul-searching processes that come from the ancient mystery schools and wisdom traditions."

My Experience:

My life brought me deep into the darkness of the unknown and the uncertain. I was brought to my knees. I experienced desperation, sadness, grief, depression, and I was tempted with hopelessness. On my knees, I was humbled, and I could completely surrender - to God. I could not give up hope. There had to be a way forward. Using my tools and empowerment from my training and progression on the Mystery School path, which included my deep connection to, and understanding of myself and God, I was able to move beyond and find joy in a whole new way of life.

My Guidance for You:

Equip yourself with all the help and support you can find, physical and spiritual – and that includes finding a true initiatory path and ancient wisdom tradition. Find some way, no matter how small, to move forward.

Never, ever, give up on yourself! Hold on as tight as you can to Hope. Seek Joy always.

Be aware of your energy output and where it is going. What

activities in your life are getting you nowhere? What in your life that requires energy from you is taking you nowhere? Find your Joy and put your energy there! Allow yourself to be happy.

There are ancient Viking symbols, known as runes, and one of them tells us: "Be certain that you are not suffering over your suffering. For it is in letting go of the past that you reclaim your power."

– Ralph Blum, "The Book of Runes"

Carla's Pearls

"I am not my physical body."

"Never give up hope."

"One step at a time."

"Life is not perfect. It's not meant to be."

"Just do what you can and love yourself through it. It's OK."

SONG

"DON'T YOU WORRY 'BOUT A THING" – Tori Kelly, SING Motion Picture

https://www.youtube.com/watch?v=t8tv38egpx8

What Did You Learn About Yourself from This Chapter?

[Write about it here]

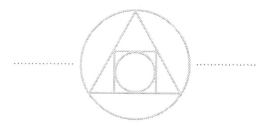

CHAPTER 6

The Alchemy of Know Thyself:

The Modern Mystery School & Lineage of King Salomon

Distillation

(Rising higher)

In this chapter, you will gain insight into an accelerated path of self-transformation and how you can use that to rise higher.

Throughout this book, I have shared how my own spiritual progression has weaved itself through my life, and I loosely related my life experiences with the stages and concepts of alchemical transformation. (There are seven stages, so we have two more to go!) In chapter 4, I described how finding a spiritual path and a guide helped me to accelerate my progression. Finally, in the previous chapter, I shared about how my experience with the Mystery School path helped me at a time when deep healing and inner transformation was needed. In this chapter, I'd like to share more about this idea of having a path to support our progression, and specifically about the Modern Mystery School, and what that really means. Do we need it? And if so, why?

I have talked about my experience of going through the chaos of the unknown and the uncertain, and how chaos is a part of transformation. If we have a map to follow, or some guidelines, we can navigate our way through chaos a little easier. Having a map and some direction adds some order and direction amid the chaos. We can move forward, through the chaos, faster. This is exactly what having a path does. A path gives us a way to create order within chaos. We all experience some degree of chaos in life, so wouldn't it be nice to have some kind of blueprint for navigating through that?

My life experience has shown me that it most definitely helps. Being a Virgo and a scientist, I have always loved order! Before I found the Modern Mystery School, I think I did a pretty good job finding and creating order in the chaos of my life. However, from the time I had my life activation, through my multiple initiations over the years, to the present day, my clarity and capability to do that, to create some order for myself in the chaos of my life, has magnified and expanded. This has brought me an inner peace and tranquility that has served me well. Do I have tranquility in every moment of every day? Oh, my Goddess, no! There are people and situations that take me off my center – much less often now, and for shorter periods of time - but they are still there. This is life. I am human. I am not perfect. That's why I need a path.

Maybe this has never happened to you, but I've been judged by other people. I have been called a wonderful mother, a neglectful mother, a hero, a bitch, a genius, a fool, etc. What if I believed them all? Furthermore, would you want your child to believe everything that other people tell them? Of course not! We want our children to know their beauty, to know their goodness, and to grow in that. And if we love ourselves enough, we want that too. In order to have that, we need the strength that is found in truly knowing ourselves.

A true, ancient path of progression is a path to Know Thyself, to come to know the truth about oneself. Why is that important? I just gave you one example from my own experience, and here's some expansion on that. In life, there are so many different kinds of circumstances that can take us off our center, i.e., out of our self-confidence or our sense of self-worth, out of connection with our goodness. When these arise for me, and begin to pull me off my center, first of all, I'm very aware of it. Then, I can look at myself. I can ask myself what the truth is about myself. The more I know myself, the easier and faster it is to bring myself back to center – to begin to see the truth of the situation I'm facing and guide myself through it. I'm bringing myself back to my center. The *especially* challenging situations used to take me days, weeks, or longer to get through, but now it might be a couple hours or even less.

Another important piece of knowing thyself has to do with our worthiness. Sometimes we don't even seek progression because we know we need healing, and we think we need to take care of that first. Then, maybe we don't seek healing because, on some level, we don't feel worthy, so we don't prioritize it. There could be many possible reasons for that, but the reasons don't really matter. What matters is taking a step, one step, in the direction of healing. Most people have no idea where to start. I'm here to tell you that real healing is possible, and you ARE worthy. And if you'd like to explore that for yourself, there's a path for that!

We can all benefit from this journey called Know Thyself. In fact, there have always been mystery schools on the planet whose sole purpose is to anchor and hold the knowledge and tools that humanity needs to do this – to progress forward. There are currently seven mystery schools on the planet, and that's why they're here. They each anchor a very ancient lineage of knowledge, tools, and power held within their initiatory path. Up until 1997, they have all remained closed, meaning not everyone could have access to them. All the knowledge and tools were held "secret". If a typical human wanted to know more about life and humanity's path of progression, and about enhancing their own life experience, they were essentially on a solitary mission. That's how humanity has been operating, for the most part, since – forever. Until 1997.

What changed? Well, humanity is changing. More and more people are looking for answers to the age-old questions of life. Who am I really? Why are we here? Is this all there is? Is there life after…life? More and more people are searching for someone or something to "show them the way". Humanity's consciousness is looking beyond religion for faith, hope, peace, and love. But it's not just that. This time on the planet, the 21st century A.D., is a time that many prophets and lineages have understood to be a very special time for mankind – a significant time in the progression of humanity. And we need help. And we've been ready to receive that help.

The mystery schools of the planet hold ancient wisdom for the progression of humanity, everything humanity needs to move forward. Moving forward means that humanity can progress to making the world a better place. It's not just random that the mission of the mystery schools is to bring peace to Earth. It's time.

Nearly 30 years ago, one man was offered a mission, with the message that we had entered a time of "No more secrets". He made a choice and accepted the mission. Following that choice, in 1997, he opened the doors of the North American Mystery School lineage to the public. He founded what we know today as the Modern Mystery School, being what is called a lineage key holder as Head Ipsissimus in the Lineage of King Salomon. Who is he? His name is Gudni Gudnason. His legacy is mammoth. I encourage you to discover more about that for yourself by visiting the Modern Mystery School's website, speaking with any Mystery School Guide, or attending any class that the Modern Mystery School offers around the world.

Now, because of this man's choice and work, the doors of this ancient lineage are open around the world, available to *anyone* who seeks progression. In 2017, two men who greatly assisted in this work, also reached the initiatory level of Ipsissimus. These three men are collectively known as The Third Order, and unitedly they hold the lineage keys. With the establishment of the Third Order, a Council of Twelve women was also formed and activated to work jointly with them, all playing a crucial role in the strength of this lineage.

What does **"lineage"** mean? Most of us understand lineage as a family line and ancestry. If you've done training in reiki healing or yoga practice, you most likely learned that the training you were receiving was part of an ancient lineage - a line of masters that ensured the integrity of the training – so that you were able to receive this same ancient training and authority in the modern world. Lineage is a way of doing things. Quite simply, lineage is a line. A line through the ages - lineage. A line of people that can be traced through the ages maintaining a certain way of doing things.

With regard to the seven mystery schools on our planet,

lineage means that teachings and empowerment are handed down from teacher to student through a sacred process of initiation. Since the beginning of time, this direct handing down of teaching has contained knowledge about God, the universe, and the role of humanity in relation to that. The Modern Mystery School, specifically, holds the lineage of King Salomon. It is the only full lineage mystery school open to the public. There are many reasons why it is called the lineage of King Salomon, but actually, it can be traced back much farther than that great and wise man who lived over three thousand years ago. This lineage is a Hermetic lineage, tracing back eight thousand years to the time of Hermes Trismegistus (who is said to have written the Emerald Tablet and the Corpus Hermeticum, two highly influential, ancient treatises). All ancient mystery schools have illuminated the path to Know Thyself. To know thyself is a Hermetic path.

Hermetic is a word that is used today when speaking about a container or a space being completely closed off to its environment. For example, in a laboratory, a hermetically sealed container may be used to prevent the outside air from contaminating what is inside, to keep it pure. It is impervious to external influence; it is airtight. When something is hermetically sealed, it cannot be acted upon by an outside force; it is unchangeable. To say that a lineage is a Hermetic lineage means, in part, that the knowledge, tools, and power held within it cannot be changed by anyone's opinion and remain good for all people at all times. It also means that there is a path – a path that allows for growth, progression, and a life of greater purpose and meaning – a path to know thyself.

When we study Hermetics, we are exploring the seven Hermetic principles of the universe. These principles are unmalleable and unchangeable. The greater our understanding of these principles, the more we come to Know Thyself, and the more empowered we become in our lives. This is Hermetics. For a very clear, empowering, and contemporary treatise on the principles of Hermetics and how to apply them in your life today, I highly recommend the book, "You Are Not Perfect The Way You Are: 11 Keys To Master Your Life.", by lineage key holder Ipsissimus Dave Lanyon.

One of many supportive things we learn is that we are either moving forward or moving backward. There is no standing still. (One of the seven hermetic principles tells us that "everything moves". Physics tells us this too.) To move forward, the path of spiritual progression is a path of initiation – rites of passage. This has always been the way of humanity - marking our progression with the ceremonies of true initiations. Over time, this process of progression has been essentially lost. Luckily for us, mystery schools have held the path for us.

The Modern Mystery School, as the lineage of King Salomon, provides "advanced spiritual training" for anyone who seeks it, i.e., open to the public, and holds a Hermetic path of progression. There are foundational teachings (like the Empower Thyself initiation class that I spoke about in chapter 4) that allow you to then study in more specialized areas of your choosing like Healers' Academies, Alchemy, Kabbalah, Sacred Geometry, Wicca, and many others. To *seek* advanced spiritual training is to seek a deeper understanding of how we can live our best lives here in the physical.

To *receive* advanced spiritual training is to become more self-aware and bring more light – more purity and goodness – into your life. It supports your own alchemical transformation process to be the best version of you. With this training, there's only one pace at which you can go, and that is your own! It is *your* path. The hermetic lineage and path is here, and now open, to support humanity – to assist us in creating a better world. Its purpose will not change, and you can choose *your* path within it. As individuals, we are all unique, with a very unique purpose, and only you can discover what that is. The mystery school path is here to help you do that.

It's all about making your life better. If you don't want to make your life better, then there's nobody or nothing that can do that for you. Maybe you're satisfied with your life just the way it is. All the magick, all the tools, all the teaching, all the healings, are all about making your life better. But it's your choice.

Now, it may not be easy. In fact, it isn't. (Maybe you learned in the last chapter that you don't necessarily want everything to be easy.) But it sure is fun! And being around a bunch of other people who are working to make their lives better, and make the world a better place, just like you are, is very joyful!

You may choose to be like the man in The Matrix movie who decides that he would rather enjoy the illusion of eating steak, and just remain a human in the matrix. We all have that choice. (The Matrix reference was discussed on page 100.)

You may be wondering how this path is any different from all the self-help books and empowerment programs; there are so many out there. You may have found great help from working with some of them. Even beyond books and programs, there are so many ways the matrix world can offer you for gaining a deeper spiritual understanding or having an amazing "spiritual experience". Please explore them with discernment. A good rule of thumb that I like to share with my students is to ask yourself, "Is this empowering me? Is this helping me to feel more empowered and in control of my life? Do I feel like I'm moving forward?". If so, great. Always pay attention to the "fruits" of your pursuits. Did it bear fruit for you? Was it good fruit or rotten fruit?

My experience has been that anything the matrix world offered me, even if it did help me for a time, to move forward in some way, always brought me to a point where there was nothing more for me. Then it was about moving on and looking for the next thing that could help me progress. On the mystery school path, I was waiting for that time to come again, not really comprehending the nature of a true ancient lineage path of progression, or the power of initiation. That time never came. I was continuing to reap good fruit. There's always more!

Whenever you get that feeling that there must be something more, and you find yourself endlessly searching in the New Age or Self-Help sections of bookstores and the internet, it means you're ready for a deeper understanding of life and yourself. You are seeking. There's a path for that! It's a path of self-mastery. It's called the true spiritual progression of an initiatory path, and that door is now open for anyone who seeks to explore. No more secrets.

So why is **initiation** so important? The ceremony of initiation, which is both physical and energetic, is a very ancient process. It allows for the power and authority of an ancient lineage to be transferred from teacher to student. Receiving initiation allows us to hold and flow more light, more goodness, the energy of God, in our lives. We become more empowered. We literally have more of the power of God flowing through us. We can truly live a more magickal life!

With initiation, we also gain a Guide. A Guide is a physical, human person who has the training and authority within the lineage to initiate you into it. The relationship we have with a physical Guide is very meaningful because they can support our spiritual progression and, at the same time, understand our very physical challenges. Over the years, my appreciation for my Guide has grown enormously. Now, being a Guide myself, I understand very clearly how valuable, and indeed necessary, it is to have a Guide. Sometimes we think we don't need any help, that we're good on our own. I have definitely been there. However, I have learned that we can only take ourselves so far when we progress alone. At some point, we need a Guide. Why not make it easier for yourself and get a Guide?

If you'd like to read some real-life stories written by real-life people who have had varying degrees of experience with the healings, tools, initiations, and teachings of the Modern Mystery School in dealing with varying life challenges, I highly recommend the book, "Ancient Healings, Modern Miracles", by Dawn Ressel. It is filled with stories of many people in various situations that were keeping them from moving forward and how they found help in overcoming them. You just might find a story that speaks to you, and in some way helps you.

Now here's something to make you laugh! At one of the first international programs I ever attended with the Modern Mystery School, there were crowds of people in the hallways during registration times, breaks and lunch. I looked around and noticed that everyone was so happy! I love happy people, I was a happy person, but there was something different going on. I remember thinking, "Normal people are not that happy!". And I was just a little bit uncomfortable. At first, I didn't really want to be like them. I was judging them to some extent, not believing it was for real. I found myself wondering how others might judge *me* if I dared to be like them. But over time, I came to realize that it was real, and I *did* want to be like them. I wanted what they had. Now I know that "average" people are not that happy. You are not average! You can be that happy!

In my progression on the path, I have come to find the people I work alongside in the Modern Mystery School to be the most honest, sincere, caring, and brave people I have ever known.

(Sure, there are weird ones in every bunch, but I've always liked the weird ones; I think I might be one of them...) Now, when we're all at international programs, crowding in the halls, smiling, and hugging each other, I just walk around with a big smile on my face thinking, "We are all happy crazy people!". And I love it!

Ok. I've used the word **"magick"** a few times now, so I thought I'd share a bit about what that means. You're probably asking, "Why is there a "k" at the end?". Well interestingly, Oxford Dictionary defines "magick" as: "archaic spelling of magic.". Somewhere along the way, we've lost the "k". I find that interesting because, in the mystery school, we learn that the "k" stands for keys. In true magick, there are keys. These keys can open doors that can take us further in our progression. And we, humanity, *have* lost them, just like the "k". More interesting, I think, is that most people today would say magic means the world of illusion. But true magick is our toolbox for getting *out* of the illusions – the illusions of the world and the illusions of our mind, out of the matrix. True magick has never really been lost; the mystery schools on the planet have always held it for us.

What is "true magick"? It is not something that happens to you. Magick is something that we do. We change something into something else. Or we create something from nothing. <u>We</u> do that. We are the magicians of our own lives. Real magick, true magick, brings in Light to make a change. It helps us change into something greater by uncovering the greatness within us! That's why when we see things happen that are good or beautiful or amazing, that we didn't expect, or that fill us with joy or awe, we call it magickal. With true magick, we, individually, can transform our own lives. We, collectively, can transform the world. As Willy Wonka said, "We are the music makers, and we are the dreamers of dreams.".

Our toolbox of magick has many tools within it. You may be surprised to learn that magick includes both science and spirituality. The reality is, we are both physical and spiritual; it makes sense that our tools would work for and with both. We need both. For example, two of our tools, the study of Alchemy and the study of Kabbalah, each hold both science and spirituality within them. When most people think of Alchemy, they think of the scientist working in a lab with the tools of chemistry. Already through this book, you're seeing some of the spiritual aspects of Alchemy and transformation, beyond the physical aspects. Alchemy is both. In Kabbalah, we study God through the tree of life, which also holds the pattern for our DNA. Magick and metaphysics have structure.

We have within us both logic (science/philosophy) and also inner knowing (spirituality/religion). Science involves trial and error and direct experience, and our knowing through science has a logic to it. Inner knowing also comes from our own direct experience, but we come to know something even if it doesn't make logical sense. I am reminded of the structure of our brain, and how the left and right hemispheres are quite different – in their structure and their function. The left-brain processes reading, writing, and calculations, and is often called the logical side of the brain. The right brain is more visual and deals in images more than words and can process much faster. So, sometimes things make logical sense to us, and sometimes, through different processing, we just know. Ideally, we are operating in the middle and utilizing all of it.

In Hermetics, there is science and logic to our knowing, but also, through our study of Hermetics and our progression in life, especially with the assistance of a path and a Guide, we can come to an inner knowing – specifically to Know Thyself. Hermes Trismegistus was considered a mystic. He spoke about the human soul. He said that one of the great diseases of the human soul is Godlessness. When I first heard that, the idea that we can have disease in our soul was a new one for me. But I have always understood the existence of God. I have understood, from both my logic and my inner knowing, the importance of God, some concept of a higher power and a higher intelligence. I have always felt connected to an all-loving God who created me in his/her own image. I feel most connected when I am in gratitude. I know I have God in me, and I am in God. I pray every day. From that perspective, I can imagine the torment of a soul who does not feel that.

Acknowledging a connection to God, some relationship with God, has saved many souls. Yet, in this world, there are many souls, many people, who continue to struggle and indeed suffer. We can help, especially If we understand that we have the power of God within us, to any degree. In fact, we are far more powerful than we know. Sometimes we wish that we could do more. The reality is that the more we help ourselves to progress into our *own* empowerment, on the path of initiation, the more power, literally, that we have to make a difference - not just in our own lives – but to make a difference in the world.

In my story over the first five chapters of this book, you learned about some of my experiences with God and spirituality, and you read about some of my "spiritual experiences". I'd like to mention something in general about spiritual experiences: A spiritual experience is not a destination. It's not the goal. It's just something that happens along the way of your progression forward. These experiences themselves are not the goal. It's kind of like a child always wanting to see over the windowsill. Finally, he can stand and pull himself up and see what's out the window. But that doesn't mean that's where he stays. He has had that experience <u>because</u> of his progression. But then he continues on, to have more and more experiences that are a result of his progression and moving forward.

I am not anyone special because of my "spiritual experiences". We all have our own path. I have noticed that many people today are seeking to have "an experience". This is really not the goal. Then, if they have one, it sometimes feeds into their identity. They believe they have become something because of an experience they had. The experience may have propelled them forward in their spiritual progression, which is great. But if so, it's a moment, a point on their path. It generally isn't helpful to attempt to repeat it over and over believing that "this is the way", or that repeating the experience has some ongoing purpose in spiritual progression. Often, it becomes an obstruction to moving forward.

Having said all that, yes, life is about having fun! It's about seeking new experiences in this amazing playground of the physical world! Enjoy it! You want to learn something new about yourself? Climb a mountain, go fishing, take care of a baby or an elderly person, explore a new country, culture, or language, row a boat out on the open water, or jump out of an airplane. Just remember, we are on a journey. Sometimes on our journey, we might pull the car over to visit a circus, or an amusement park, and that's part of our journey, and it's awesome. But then it's time to get back in the car, back on the road, back on the path moving forward.

Most importantly, always remember that *we are already spirit*! Spirit is our living essence. We are not simply physical beings seeking a spiritual experience. We already are *spiritual* beings, and we are having a *physical* experience, not the other way around.

WHAT IS HEALING?

No matter where we are on our own individual path, we can all benefit from healing. You might ask, "Why is that?". Well, let's first talk about what healing is. Conventionally, in modern western medicine, healing has meant treating the physical body when it's ill or injured. As humanity has progressed, the world has begun to look at healing from a more expanded perspective. When I was growing up, it was becoming more popular for people to pay attention to their mental health, in addition to their physical body health. It became much more commonplace for people to seek psychological counseling and support, and today, it's not uncommon for even children to receive mental health care.

So, we have advanced somewhat in understanding the needs of our bodies and our minds to keep them functioning well. Now, we're also beginning, more and more, to explore the concept of "body, mind and spirit". Body and mind, check – to some degree. What about spirit? Hermes talked about diseases of the soul. That was a new idea for me, but I have learned a lot. From Mystery School teachings, our soul is related to our body, and our mind, and our spirit. That would seem to make it pretty important. So, if our soul could have disease or illness, we would probably want to know a little more about how to take care of that.

Guess what? In the Mystery School, we have an advanced understanding of what it means to heal the soul. As it turns out, healing for the soul is a big part of "advanced spiritual training" – and it can be pretty advanced. In fact, in ancient times and in many ancient civilizations, there was a knowledge and an understanding that healing included body, mind and spirit. What's more, it was only a few hundred years ago when the wisdom of Alchemy was used to heal many diseases of man - healing with an acknowledgment of all three aspects of our being. Because we ARE all of it. When we begin to understand the inter-relatedness of the physical body, the mind, the soul, and the spirit, we can begin to heal ALL that makes us, well, us.

And if healing ourselves and advancing on the initiatory path can really bring us the empowerment we need to not only make our own lives better, but the lives of others, then all of this "advanced spiritual training" seems like exactly what we need to make the world a better place. It sounds pretty "spot on" for alleviating much of the suffering in the world and moving many more people into finding and creating their own fulfillment in life!

PURPOSE AND MISSION

Fulfillment is a word worth exploring. What does it mean to be fulfilled? In my story, I found fulfillment in my life from many things, including being a chemist, being a mother, and my work as a neonatologist. Once I stepped onto the mystery school path, I discovered that there can always be more! I went on to find more fulfillment than ever before when I began healing, teaching, and guiding others to find more of their own fulfillment. From my experience, fulfillment is tied to purpose. When we feel that we are serving our purpose, we find fulfillment. And it usually does involve serving others. Again, in my story, I grew up understanding the importance of service to others. But simply being in service to others, while it is a wonderful and meaningful thing to do, does not mean that you are necessarily in alignment with your purpose.

Purpose is known in our soul. When we are serving our purpose, our soul is satisfied, and we feel fulfilled. I felt very satisfied, at a soul level, when I was working as a neonatologist. My body wasn't very satisfied because I hadn't yet learned to serve myself first, but I *knew* that it was my purpose. Then, I found that there could be *more* to my purpose, that I could find even more fulfillment in life.

I have some musings to share about this idea of purpose. What is purpose? What is my purpose? What defines me?

If I am a doctor, I am fulfilling the purpose of a doctor. If I am a bread maker, I am fulfilling the purpose of a bread maker – to make bread. What is the purpose of a cashier? I can step into that role and when I do that, my purpose in those moments is to serve the purpose of being a cashier. But is that <u>my</u> purpose? What is the purpose of Carla Weis? Perhaps it is to serve the purpose of being a doctor, a scientist, a writer, a mother, but what makes me unique? Do I let those identities define me? What *does* define me? And so, I ask you, what defines you? What is *your* purpose? Is the world or your society defining who you are? If you don't consider these things then, by default, they are.

One could say that purpose is part of a mission. If I have a specific mission that I am passionate about, then everything I do has a purpose that is in alignment with that mission. But still, I have to ask myself, "Is this what Carla Weis is here to do? Is this really feeding my soul? In my own progression, I have found that I can most clearly answer these kinds of questions the more I come to truly know myself. Who am I? The only person who can answer that question is me. No one, absolutely no one, can tell me exactly who *I* am. Or what my purpose is. I have learned not to give the power of defining who I am to anyone or anything outside of myself.

However, walking forward on the Mystery School path, with the teachings, tools, and initiations, has assisted me tremendously in answering those questions for myself.

I now know that *my* purpose is in alignment with the purpose of humanity, and the heart's desire of the collective to align with God and create a better world, a world of peace and harmony. Actually, it always has been. But now I have found a way to align with that on a higher level. (Remember, there's always more, if we choose it.) Now I ask you, "What defines you? Does the outside world define you? How well do you know yourself? If you would like to explore more about that, it's here and it's real.

If that doesn't interest you, maybe you've already found your nirvana. In my experience with glimpsing a sense of unity with God, it has always led me to move myself forward, towards more of that, and ultimately it has led me to do whatever I can to help others create a better life for themselves.

Or maybe, you just don't believe it's possible. I invite you - for just a second - to ask yourself, "What if it was?". Is it worth exploring? Or maybe, somewhere deep inside, you're just stopping yourself. If so, why is that? Know that you are worthy of all good things.

And finally, there's the circumstance where you *do* believe it's possible. Maybe you can appreciate the possibility that others can have these experiences and find their purpose and fulfillment in life, but for some reason it's not possible for you. Of course, it is! But you have to believe that. And more importantly, you have to take some action to try and find out. The more worthy you feel within yourself, the easier it is to take that action.

What if others think you're off your rocker? Throughout my life, many people have told me that, and many more people have thought that about me. But I had to find out for myself. What if I believed the people who said that I couldn't be a doctor and also have children? It's tempting to believe them, but we all need to search and find out for ourselves what's possible. How else would we really know for sure? Otherwise, the opinions of others can drag us down or simply keep us from moving forward.

There's an interesting observation about crabs – yes, the sea creatures we call crabs. (Maybe you know about it.) When I was young, my cousins and I would go crabbing, and I observed this phenomenon for myself. If you put a bunch of crabs in a bucket or an open box, you never have to worry about them escaping. You don't have to put any cover on the container. They won't get out. That's because if one of them begins to climb out, which they do, all the other crabs will pull them back down. It never fails. So please, in *whatever* you do in this world, don't let the other crabs keep you trapped. Maybe *your* purpose requires you to get out of the box. Find your uniqueness, and don't be afraid to just be you. Years ago, my daughter, Jaime, used to always tell me, "You do you, Mom." It has never failed me. This is not about anybody else's life. It's about *your* life. And you get out of it what you choose to put into it.

You can do what I did when I first stepped onto this path. Just dip your toes in and see what it feels like. Get a life activation. Or just talk to a Guide in the Modern Mystery School and ask them a million questions. Find out for yourself. Make a choice to do something for yourself that just might change your life! As they say, "Shoot for the moon. Even if you miss, you'll land among the stars!". Just make sure that you are making choices based on your own experience and your own due diligence, not something that you've read online or heard from others. Remember, it's so important to find out for yourself, from your *own* experience.

If you are someone who has already taken a step or two, or more, on the Mystery School path, ask yourself, "What's my next step?". Then talk to your Guide and figure out what would serve you best. Finally, make some choice to do something to assist yourself in moving forward in some way.

Physically and spiritually, I have probably been on this path a bit longer than you have. In my physical life, that's probable, and in my spiritual progression, it's most likely. Either way, chances are pretty good that I have been around a little longer than you have. I am a little further down the road and that means that I can help you. In fact, *any* of the MMS Guides can do that. When it comes to spiritual progression, physical age means very little. Any one of us can help you get just a little further down your road.

In our physical life, we're all moving further down the road, whether we like it or not. But moving further down the road of our spiritual progression is a choice. I made the choice to walk down this road pretty much in tandem with my physical progression, and it has made the physical life so much more miraculous and joyful! That is possible for any of us!

As for me, I like moving forward, even if it's not always comfortable. I'm expanding. I just focus on taking one more step. That's how we change the world. One step at a time. One person at a time. And we start with ourselves – the only person we *can* change. I try to always look at myself first. "Am I serving *myself* enough? Am I loving *myself* enough?" And then, if I experience someone or something in the world that I don't like, "Where might a piece of this be inside me, and how can I change that?".

Regarding purpose and mission, I hope that you are encouraged to make a choice to move, to get just a little more in touch with your soul, to walk just a little further down your road of spiritual progression. I hope you continue to seek more clarity on what *your* unique purpose is in this world. And I hope we can all align our purpose with the larger mission of making the world a better place, in some way shape or form.

So, as I asked in the beginning of this chapter, do we need an true ancient lineage initiatory path? Collectively, we absolutely do. We always have, even if we weren't aware of it. If indeed our mission is to make the world a better place, to bring peace, then we need it. Individually, we can all greatly benefit from the path. And the only way the collective can achieve our mission is if individuals acknowledge their role, their purpose in the greater mission. For individuals to do that, and to fulfill that to any significant degree, yes, we as individuals need a path. Obviously, not every individual will choose to utilize the path, and that's fine. It is not necessary. We, collectively, can transform the world. To do that, we need a path.

The Modern Mystery School is not the only path. It is what has worked for me, and because of my experience, it is what I highly recommend.

Our mission is to bring hope, and through hope, to bring peace on earth - Shamballa. And that will bring us to the seventh and final alchemical stage and the final chapter...

Distillation

In the sixth stage of Alchemy, called Distillation, there is much further refinement. Beyond the fire of fermentation, there is continued inspiration from above. We must wash away all that is inferior to find peace and well-being, to bring us closer to perfection, closer to God. There are often many cycles of distillation that then bring further refinement.

Here, the ego is no longer dominating our behavior as we hear ever more loudly and ever more clearly the voice of our soul.

I love what Dennis William Hauck said about Distillation in "The Emerald Tablet: Alchemy for Personal Transformation":

"...the purified soul will behold its object and peer into the eye of God."

My Experience:

I have always sought to live my best life, here and now, and make the best impact I can in this world. The Modern Mystery School, holding the lineage of King Salomon, has given me the opportunity to take this aspiration to a much higher level by showing me a way to further refine myself and to "peer into the eye of God" with dependable consistency. This path has helped me in the process of washing away "all that is inferior", to keep my ego in check, and to find peace and harmony at a soul level, while I'm still here in the physical.

With regard to self-transformation, my experience with the Modern Mystery School has taught me that reaching this point would be extremely difficult to do without an initiatory path. For me, it has been the most accelerated and most facilitative path for finding what I was looking for. I am continuing to refine myself.

My Guidance:

To fund more power in your life, get in touch with your soul and make a choice to explore who you are just a little bit more. Get a life activation to "activate" your connection to yourself, to your true essence, and explore what else the Modern Mystery School has for you. Do *something* for your soul and your own empowerment. The more power we fund within our own lives, the more we can help others, and the more we can help the world.

Following a true ancient Mystery School path will support the healing and empowerment of your soul. There is a process. A path has already been laid for us in the ancient lineage of King Salomon and the administration of that through The Modern Mystery School. You don't need to reinvent the wheel.

Finally, do what every mother everywhere has always said, "Be good".

Carla's Pearls

"I am worthy."

"It's here and it's real."

"You do you." (OK, so I borrowed this from Jaime.)

"Don't let the other crabs keep you trapped."

SONG

"COME ALIVE" – The Greatest Showman Ensemble
https://www.youtube.com/watch?v=JYrc-kWEccg

What Did You Learn About Yourself from This Chapter?

[Write about it here]

CHAPTER 7

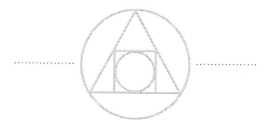

The Alchemy of Peace on Earth:

Hope for Humanity

Coagulation

(Creating unity)

In this chapter you will discover how you can find your place in the creation of unity here on Earth.

At this time on the planet, we're ready for a massive shift in our collective human consciousness, so that we can clean up and overcome the ills of our global society such as poverty, hunger, violence, drug abuse, and abuse of our planet. To do this requires magick; it requires Alchemy. Alchemy is an art and a science. Alchemy is life. Each stage of Alchemy operates on all three aspects: the physical, mental, and spiritual. Yet, it's all Alchemy of the soul.

In this book, I have shared how my spiritual progression has evolved through my life, and how the path of the Modern Mystery School has greatly accelerated and supported my progression, in all aspects of my life. You can also hear or read about so many stories from other people about their healing, recovery, and success which resulted from using the tools of this lineage, including healings, activations, and initiations. Please understand that while all of this is true, and wonderful, these are steps - steps that support the healing of the soul of humanity, to build toward our mission, to move us forward collectively.

Everything we do in the Mystery School lineage is about bringing more Light to the world, bringing hope to humanity. It is understood that through hope, we can come to know the beauty and goodness within us, individually and collectively, and find that our true essence, our eternal spirit, exists as part of the spirit of God. Furthermore, that by connecting to this divine spirit of God that dwells within us, that is our true essence, and embracing that power of God within us, we can indeed bring that which is above to the below. We can actually manifest peace, harmony, and unity among all creatures of Earth. This is the promise that we each hold within us.

Whether we understand that we hold the power of God within us or not, we all wield this power to some extent already. We do flow the Light of God into this world. Whenever we share a warm smile with someone who needs it, we are flowing the Light of God into the world – and specifically to another person. Whenever we assist people in their needs or help them in some way to manage and overcome their struggles, we are flowing the Light of God into the world and, on some level, we are helping these people awaken to the Light of God, the goodness and worthiness, within themselves. We do this all the time.

What if we all actually did understand that we hold the Light and power of God within us? Then, as we come to discover our own unique purpose in this world (which will always evolve the more we come to know ourselves), the more we could choose to simply align our purpose, our will, with the Will of God. We would be harnessing the power of God from within us to flow even more of the Light of God here on Earth.

I know many of you do this every day. If you're not already an initiate, imagine how much greater an impact you could be having in the world with the power of initiation. Remember, initiation expands your capacity to hold and harness Light and therefore flow it into the world. The initiatory path is a path of progression toward our fullest potential as a human being. We can all choose to do lightwork without an initiatory path. We can do that because Light is our true essence. If you would like to be in service on a higher level, take a step onto the path.

Service is such an important part of lightwork. To know our own goodness, our God-ness, is a crucial part of service. As I learned, we must serve ourselves first. When our cup is replete, we can overflow to others. As we move forward on the initiatory path, the Light brings empowerment, and that allows us to be in service to others on higher and higher levels. The more our cup is filled with Light, the more our desire is to share that with others.

What about this idea of healing the soul of humanity? The description that has always made the most sense to me is considering our soul as a hot air balloon. There are things that can help it rise, for example the fire, and things that can bring it down, for example sandbags. Our soul wants to rise and be lighter rather than being burdened by those things that contribute to us feeling disempowered or separate from our goodness, our true essence. So, in this analogy, the hot air balloon wants to rise. To do that, we must dispel with some of the sandbags. The sandbags of our soul represent any disturbance or discord, physical, mental, or emotional, that keeps our mind from elevating itself, from connecting with, and indeed knowing, our goodness and our eternal spirit nature.

All the tools of the Modern Mystery School are aimed toward this purpose of healing our soul. A point of clarity, our soul cannot be healed without our participation; it is always our choice to do so.

Free will is a God-given gift. Nothing and no one that operates in alignment with the Will of God can ever do anything that supersedes our own free will. So, if it is our choice to gain some of this healing, it requires us to take some action, of our own free will. Again, I highly recommend seeking a life activation session.

As I have mentioned earlier in this book (page 104), the life activation has many benefits. Ultimately, it takes the connection that we have with our true spirit essence to a much higher level. I've noticed that sometimes in our lives, we literally don't see things, either because we have some block to seeing them, or we simply don't want to see them. The connection provided by the life activation raises our vibration to a higher plane so we can begin to see things more clearly, things that were always there but were somehow being blocked from our awareness. Having our awareness expanded is one of the many benefits we can enjoy after receiving the life activation.

Over the centuries, so many people have used the empowerment of this lineage's initiatory path to make a huge impact on the world. Some examples are Aristotle, Leonardo DaVinci, William Shakespeare, Nicola Tesla, Rudolph Steiner, Carl Jung, David Bowie, and Santana. Guess what? You may have a much bigger part to play in *your* life than you think! What *is* your part to play? I hope you continue to explore that.

Consider all those who have brought powerful teachings to the world in support of humanity's progression, Jesus, Mohammed, Buddha, to name a few. Isn't it possible that they were all helping us to understand the same things? To acknowledge the power of God within us, to align with the Will of God to do good in the world, and to love our brothers and sisters? Well now, what is the Will of God? If God created this universe, and one of the laws of the universe (from both Hermetics and physics) is that everything moves, then it would appear that movement is in alignment with the Will of God. To improve, progress, or advance ourselves - to move forward - is generally considered to be a good thing while stagnation is generally considered undesirable. So, it would appear that we can view expansion, growth, and progression as being in alignment with God's will. God expanding God. Perhaps we can view all of these teachers, sometimes called Masters, as having a common purpose, to share with us the idea of expanding the Light of God in the world, and that we can all do that.

If bringing more of the Light of God into the world is in alignment with the Will of God, what about your will? Well, *your* will is the only way this can be done. Why? God lives in you. God works through you. You have goodness, God-ness. Please do not think of yourself as separate from God. You are not. Now, we don't control anyone else's will except our own (I hope). So, it is through our will, individually, and our will collectively, that we can bring more of the spirit of God, peace, harmony, love, and unity from above, here into the physical. By aligning our will with the Will of God, we can literally bring Heaven to Earth. So, shine your Light!

Shining your Light in the world may be as simple as smiling at someone. Never underestimate the power of a smile to bring hope to someone. Remember, we are all struggling with something. Sometimes a simple, joyful smile can raise someone's vibration out of whatever misery was clouding their mind, heart, or soul. (Pretend you're from California and smile at somebody!) I have found that smiling at someone can actually raise my *own* vibration when I'm not feeling my best. Of course, there are many more ways for us to shine our Light. However it is that you choose to shine your Light in the world, please keep in mind that our impact in the world is greatly augmented by progressing on an initiatory path.

One of my former hospital partners, not yet activated or initiated, often tells her children when struggles are happening, "Find the Light and move forward". She shared this with me when this book was nearly complete, and I just loved it! So, I'm sharing it here. We all inherently and intuitively know that this is good!

DIVINE FEMININE AND BALANCE

As we move forward, closer to a time of less chaos and more harmony, we must embrace the idea of balanced masculine and feminine energies on the planet - within each of them, and between the two. With regard to the divine feminine, all cultures and traditions have ways of acknowledging and working with the divine feminine. Being raised Catholic, my first experience, beyond my mother, was with the Blessed Mother Mary. Over the years, my experience with, and awareness of, this energy has expanded. It is beautiful, it is divine, and it is powerful. As they say, with great power comes great responsibility.

In this book, I have used the stages of Alchemy, to some degree, as a lens through which to view my life and my spiritual progression. We all have masculine and feminine energies within us. Through the seven stages of Alchemy, the relationship between these two energies evolves toward perfection. As I have moved through life, my understanding of how I express my divine feminine energy has evolved, and consequently, my expression of that has been refined.

My mother, my aunts, and all the females in my family have been great role models of feminine strength for me, in all forms. Even as women's roles in society evolved over the generations, I could always see a common thread among them. They have always held a reverence for God and all that which is holy, a sense of showing kindness and compassion to others, authenticity, self-confidence, and an unbridled readiness to laugh! – at ourselves and life. (Laughter runs through *all* of my family!) I've watched them have a willingness to sacrifice their own desires for the well-being of loved ones, especially for children who were fiercely loved and protected, without nuclear family boundaries. A mother to one was a mother to all!

In my own experience as a mother, I have experienced great joy! I treasure those sacred times of having an infant nursing and then sleeping on my chest while all of my senses were being so tenderly stimulated. Some of my most precious memories are of feeling my babies growing within my body, the glorious moments of holding and experiencing my newborn just after giving birth, singing lullabies to them, enjoying my girls when they were young and exploring the world around them, and then growing up and finding their places in it. Then, the experience of being a grandmother which brought a joy all its own. Beyond all of that, I have spent most of my life caring for babies and mothers.

Nonetheless, one could say that I have an interesting history with the divine feminine. I was raised in a house with three brothers and no sisters; I was "at home" with masculine energy. I then became a mother of five daughters and no sons, suddenly finding myself quite confused when I looked around at what was happening in my house. It was foreign to me in so many ways. But I learned and I adapted. Also, in every stage of my professional life, I chose to be a woman in a man's world, so to speak.

Back when I was in medical training, the surgical "scrubs" for doctors were pants and tops, and so that's what women doctors also wore. But the nurses, who were mostly women, many times wore scrub dresses. During my fellowship training, I was in a hospital where I had access to scrub dresses and so, ever since then, that's what I have always worn in the hospital, even as I became the only one doing so. Sadly, there were times I was castigated for that by female nurses, but very few. Far more often over the years, women doctors and nurses have asked me where they could get scrub dresses! (Now that I don't work in the hospital anymore, I'm wondering if there are any other female doctors, or nurses, who still wear scrub dresses. I hope so.)

I have always loved wearing dresses, and I didn't ever feel a need to <u>be</u> a man. I liked expressing myself as a woman; I just so happened to be working in a "man's world". But I could never let go of my deep connection to my femininity, my deep desire to be a mother of many children, and then my fulfillment in doing so, and my love for the divine feminine aspect of God – which I first knew in my mother, then in the Blessed Mother, and then in myself. Yet over the years, I have continued to examine my relationship with my own divine feminine and masculine aspects, how balanced they are within me, and what changes might support my empowerment. I've noticed that when doing this, it's easy to be confused. There are so many societal influences, family influences, and even our own doubts that can cloud this process.

Fortunately, I've always had a fairly strong sense of self, and so I think that I have navigated through all this reasonably well. Additionally, since I've had access to the deeper Mystery School teachings that support knowing thyself, I have gained even more clarity, and with that, came more empowerment. However, in my experience with transforming myself through the experience of chronic illness (detailed in Chapter 5), my relationship with and understanding of the divine feminine evolved quite a bit more, as did how I wield that energy within myself and out in the world.

Because of the severe energy depletion in my physical body, actively moving around in the world, even talking, was an exertion. My expression in the world was literally, and significantly, dampened. I had to face my inner world more than ever before. I experienced silence more than ever. There was often silence in my mind since even processing thoughts consumed energy. In the process of meditation, we learn to focus our mind, and we can also learn to empty our mind. Well, focused meditation became challenging, but my mind was empty a lot!

The thoughts that *would* come were more negative than positive, for example, victimhood, shame, confusion, and hopelessness. As I continued to redirect my negative thoughts, I became progressively more aware of the power of the divine feminine within me. There was an immense power in the silence of my inner world. It was very much a loving and nurturing power. I found peace in silence – not just as a meditation experience or a spiritual exercise, but as a way of life every day. I could wholeheartedly accept doing nothing with more peace than ever before. Then, when I *was* expressing my action-oriented masculine energy, there was more balance. I felt more at peace with what I could do and with what I couldn't do.

My new, enhanced connection with divine feminine energy developed from a deep desire to not suffer, a deep desire to be able-bodied enough to be in service to others, and then ultimately, from a deep desire to find a way to love myself more. Even though I could not express myself nearly as much as I would have liked, this unseen and unspoken energy within me was fiercely loving. I was able to nurture myself in a whole new way. This energy exists within ALL of us!

So now, I am very much aware that it is the divine feminine within me that lets me know when it's time to rest, when it's time to create limits and boundaries, when it's time to be kind to myself and to nurture myself. *Don't worry, my dear. Everything is going to be ok.*

Now, just a few words on the negative aspect of feminine energy. As a little girl through to adulthood, I have known what it feels like to be judged and criticized by other girls/women. Men have told me that they can see this facet of us as well, and moreover, they know well that feeling of being criticized by females. While as women, we can certainly be mean to each other, we can also be mean to men. There's just no denying it. Women know how to be mean. There are books, stage plays, and movies based on this concept. So, how do we move forward?

Well, as always, that's up to each of us individually. I continue to pay attention to my own thoughts, words, and actions to ensure I am behaving in the spirit of compassion and kindness, to both men and women. I have gotten much better at being able to identify when that idea of separateness creeps in, that often comes under the umbrella of competitiveness, and I let it go. I have no need to compete with or be mean to other women, or men. (Remember from Chapter 4: *"My only competition is myself."*)

In my own progression as a woman on the path to Know Thyself, I discovered that, unknowingly, I was seeing women as "less capable" compared to men, actually as less valuable. Perhaps this was a result of the era in which I grew up, or simply my own view of myself that I was projecting onto other women, or maybe some combination. Either way, as I came to know myself as being innately strong, capable, and valuable, I was able to view other women with that same respect. When I know longer had anything to prove to myself about myself, I no longer felt any competitiveness with other women. As I exalted myself, I came to exalt all women. Furthermore, I have become very ok with my vulnerability. I am very ok with not being perfect while we all help each other to move forward.

The more I have become conscious of all these things, the more I have witnessed my life become more joyful and more peaceful. My relationships with other women, which for the most part have always been good, have become even better and incredibly supportive. More than that, when we come together in pure acceptance of each other, we generate more joy! This is another opportunity for me to share that when we learn to let go of our judgements of others, we become less judgmental of ourselves. And that is such a good thing!

Similarly, I find no need to be mean to men. In my life, I have three brothers who would do anything to support me and the other women in their lives. I have watched them all be such strong forces of goodness and kindness in the world and support their wives and children with deep devotion. My daughters have men in their lives who have supported them in ways for which I could not be more thankful. I have seen many men show kindness and compassion. I've watched many men be nurturing and empathetic. I have also seen men be very abusive to women, *and* I have seen women be very abusive to men. Yes, these are my personal experiences, and I also have a lot of life experience that has allowed me to view the world from a broader and higher perspective.

I have come to see that each one of us hold both feminine qualities and masculine qualities with our own balance of the two, and that there are clear and distinct differences between these two qualities. Each of them can be balanced or imbalanced within us. When out of balance, they can contribute to disturbances within us, and also in the world, resulting in us holding each other back. When uniquely balanced within us, it can help to make this world a better place, regardless of our differences. As a woman, I have learned much about my own balance within, and also about letting go of any competitiveness with other women and with men. I have also come to have a deeper appreciation of the role that men play to help make this world a better place for all of us.

From the Mystery School perspective, it is never good when men hold women back *or* when women hold men back. Put more clearly, it is never good when any person holds another person back. Remember what this book is about? Moving forward. It's about moving ourselves forward, but also doing what we can to help each other move forward. The more we can all heal, and hold more kindness, love, and compassion in our hearts, for ourselves and others, the more we can move forward. All of this heals imbalances. We can <u>all</u> do this. It's our choice.

SHAMBALLA

If you look around the world today, it doesn't look much like a world that is building Shamballa, or a world of peace. Remember, chaos is a necessary part of transformation. We <u>are</u> heading in the right direction, but we need more of the collective to shift in order for us to create more momentum, more dynamic and consistent movement in that direction.

There is hope. Don't buy into the rhetoric that the world is falling apart. Chaos being a part of transformation means that things falling apart is simply a stage in our progression. Yes, some old forms may need to be dismantled and new ones built, but beyond falling apart, there is more. And there is a better world. Every religion and spiritual tradition speaks of a time when we return to peace. So don't focus on the rhetoric. Focus on doing the work of bringing in more Light. Ask, "What can I do to help?".

The world *is* changing. More and more, people are acknowledging self-care and empathy for others. People are valuing unity and understanding more. You're probably not going to see it reported on the news or on social media, but humanity is moving forward. We are changing. We are evolving...in the direction of Shamballa.

It all depends on what <u>we</u> do. Or what we don't do. We can pray, and prayer is essential, but we must not wait for someone else to do something. We must do less criticizing of others and more problem-solving through action. Essentially, it all depends on us. What do we want? What do <u>you</u> want? I know what I want. I want *all* people to feel safe, nourished, healed, and also to experience the fulfillment and joy of being aligned with their unique purpose. If enough of us can do this individually, then the collective of humanity – and indeed the world – can find that. We call that Shamballa.

The Modern Mystery School, which holds the lineage of King Salomon, exists for just this purpose. The teachings, tools, and empowerment of the lineage hold everything we need to make this shift. We shift by putting effort into healing ourselves, coming to know ourselves on the deepest and highest levels, and creating peace and harmony within. All it takes is for us to simply do a little better today than we did yesterday, moving just a little bit farther along our path of progression. As I like to say, we change the world one person at a time, and we start with ourself.

What we are really doing is bringing spirit into the physical, or perhaps more accurately, awakening spirit within the physical. That spirit is God. God is here. We can see God every day. We can see God every time we look into the eyes of someone we love or someone who is helping us in a time of need; we can hear God in the voice of someone offering us reassurance. Yet are we really connecting to that power within us? Sometimes it's easier for us to see God and goodness in the eyes of others than in our own eyes. When we look in the mirror, do we see someone we love? The founder of the Modern Mystery School, Gudni Gudnason, has shared the practice of looking at himself in the mirror and repeating, "I love you", for up to fifteen minutes. I have found this practice so insightful and so supportive. I say "I love you" to myself all the time!

Shamballa is not a foregone conclusion. We must create it. Shamballa will come from each of us strengthening our connection to God. It will come from us identifying with, honoring, and aligning with the Good and Goodness - the God-ness within us – within you and me.

One very simple and straightforward thing we can all do is to pay attention to where we are judging others *and* where we are judging ourselves. We all have good intentions. We are all, in essence, good people. Yet so much separation comes from our judgments and our opinions. Can we just not judge anyone? Including ourselves?

We all have our own unique perceptions, the veils through which we see and experience people and situations in the world, and they can shade or color the way we see, but also how we choose to respond to people and situations. Often, we jump to judge other people. If we can open our mind to the perception of others, understanding that it may be very different from our own, we may see things a little differently. There is an old adage, "Never judge a person until you've walked a mile in their shoes.". Keeping this in mind is a simple thing we can do that can make all the difference.

When I was growing up, my father taught me that the Golden Rule is to treat everyone the way you would like to be treated. Both of my parents have embodied this. Let's all just start with that.

The goal is to move our conscious awareness into more unity and less separation. As a doctor, over many years of training and practicing, I learned to take care of other humans, all of them, as if they were my family. Through my work, I came to see the raw humanness in everyone, young and old. And it had nothing to do with what they had or hadn't done in their life, or what they believed or didn't believe. It had to do with how alike we all are. How much can you see yourself in others?

We truly are all connected. We all play some part in the lives of others and vice versa. I would not be who I am and what I am in this world today without my parents, my teachers, my family, my friends, and on and on. They have all played a part in my progression in life in some way. Hopefully I have played a part in their lives which supported them, but either way, I know that I played some role for them.

So you see, we are all intertwined and connected. When we can focus *less* on our judging and blaming, less on our differences, and *more* on our similarities, on how we can make it better, how we can support each other, the world becomes a better place. Can you see yourself in others? Everyone can use more kindness and compassion, and more of what makes the world a better place. It is in our own healing, through kindness and compassion for ourselves and for others, that we all can move forward to create more of a force of good in this world. We are all literally just walking each other home.

I'm writing this chapter in mid-December. In the Northern Hemisphere, we have the Winter Solstice, the shortest day and the longest night. Whatever your tradition, it is a time of acknowledging and celebrating the return and expansion of light in the world to dispel the darkness, and the promise of Joy and Peace on Earth.

It's a time of year when we recognize what's really important, and when our faith in humankind is restored. I've always wondered why people can so readily accept this idea of joy and peace in the world during this season, but during the rest of the year, it simply becomes a Pollyanna idea. Can we hold this celebration of light and hope and joy in our hearts all year long? I think there's a song about that.

There's another seasonal song that speaks of a day when we will all be free. From the Mystery School's perspective, true freedom is to liberate the mind. It's not about religion or politics or money or any particular truth. The only truth we can find is that of truly knowing ourselves. Reality is always changing. Anyway, it's not really truth that people care about. People care about, "Does anybody really love me?", "Where's my next paycheck coming from?", and "How can I get out from under this pressure?". Let's be a container of hope and support for others.

It is *my* hope that from this season of Light, we can all continue to awaken to the Light that we hold within us. That with every passing season, we can hold onto that Light, nurture it, and cultivate it, until there is so much Light in the world that everyone can find Joy and Light in Life!

In the 1970's there was a very popular song called Shambala, by Three Dog Night. You've probably heard it. (You might want to listen to it again while you read the lyrics.) Incidentally, Shamballa has several different spellings. It doesn't matter how we spell it, or even what we call it – Shangri-La, Garden of Eden, paradise, peace on Earth, etc. All that matters is that we believe world peace is possible, and that we focus our energy in that direction. Equally important is understanding that you're not just believing in world peace, you're believing in the goodness of yourself; you're believing in the goodness of humanity.

Let's talk a little bit about what world peace could look like, and the difference between "peace" and "comfort". With the idea of world peace, we have harmony, compassion, and a sense of unity. But that doesn't mean there wouldn't still be challenges. There would still be things for us to move through, and things to move forward towards. As opposed to comfort. When we are comfortable, we prefer not to move. We prefer not to leave a state of comfort for a state of discomfort, even though that is what is required for our growth.

Peace doesn't mean no challenge, no struggle, no growth. There can be a lot of growth in times of peace and harmony. Peace and harmony facilitate growth. Alternatively, comfort does not support growth. Of course, we all need the comfort of a home, security, safety, a foundation of comfort upon which we can grow. However, if we remain in the comfort of our home, how could we ever experience the world, live, learn, and grow?

When it comes to world peace, it is about win-win solutions where everyone benefits, and it all comes down to choices. What choices are we making collectively? What choices are we making individually? What kind of a world do you want to live in? What choice will you make?

There **is** a path to world peace. It is a path of progression and empowerment for the masses of humanity. It's a path that has always been here for us within the mystery school traditions. It is now open to the public...because we are ready. We are ready to move into a world without war and suffering. This is the path that will get us there. It won't come from the human mind. It has to come from a connection to God that is not defined or segregated by the human mind.

It may not be you who walks this path. Someone who has walked this path may help you or guide you or influence you in some way; maybe they already have. You may have found another path, or maybe you're just struggling to survive. There is hope. As long as we are collectively moving forward in the direction of unity and peace, it is good.

There is a higher power that most of us call God and the Will of God. This power can be used in the world for good. We can harness that power within ourselves and create good and lasting changes in the world. There is a path to accelerate this process, if you choose to participate. We **can** witness the birth of a new and beautiful world!

One of the easiest ways to connect with God is through the simple practice of gratitude. And so, I would like to thank you for reading this book. I truly hope that these words and pages have guided you to find some connection with your soul and have ignited a flame of possibility within your heart. Please let me know how I can help guide you as you take your next step in moving forward. You are not alone. We all have so many wonderful things to explore and experience together!

I love you all!

Coagulation

In the seventh stage of Alchemy, Coagulation, we have come full circle, yet we are completely transformed. The completion of this cycle yields what is called the Philosophers Stone, which is incorruptible and all-powerful, and able to change any metal into gold.

Yes, colloquially, Alchemy is about changing lead to gold. When we work with Alchemy in our own life, it can be said that we are transforming the heaviness of our soul to a perfected form, balanced and united, with a unity consciousness. This is often the goal of alchemists and mystics alike.

Alchemy is life. We are in the crucible. The goal for humanity is to evolve as a collective into our perfected existence here on Earth.

My Comments:

I am not using the caption "My Experience" here, as I did in the previous chapters, since I do not consider myself to be in a perfected state. I am not perfect, but I do what I can to move in that direction – I am perfect because I am progressing toward perfection. (As written by Ipsissimus Dave Lanyon in the book, "You Are Not Perfect The Way You Are".)

In Chapter 5, I said that I felt like a phoenix rising from the ashes. That analogy is also often applied to this final stage of Alchemy. I do feel like a butterfly emerging from the chrysalis. My wings are still a little wet and I'm getting reoriented, trying to figure out where I go from here. I can fly.

I am a Goddess of the sea. I am Aphrodite.
I am still wet and sticky, finding that I have wings.
I am the goddess emerging.
And unaware of my true beauty, I fly high...
A Goddess flowing in all her beauty and goodness.

My Guidance:

Express your goodness in the world. Shine your Light!

Instead of impulsively jumping to judge others, help others who are struggling.

Pay attention to your thoughts and redirect them to

expressing love and compassion for yourself, and for others. What would God do?

Remember gratitude.

Carla's Pearls

"I am Good."

"How can I help you?"

"If the name of the game is Live and Learn, then the game gets better with: LIVE, LOVE AND LEARN."

"We change the world one person at a time, and we start with ourselves. If I am better, the world is better."

And now it's time to move forward in the cycle of transformation, a circle has no end. We can always surrender again to the fire of calcination. For we can always be in our process of transformation and moving forward, moving closer to God.

SONGS

"ONE TRIBE" – Black Eyed Peas

https://www.youtube.com/watch?v=D8nF7-hlFuY

"HEAL THE WORLD" – Michael Jackson

https://www.youtube.com/watch?v=BWf-eARnf6U

"ETERNAL BEING" – Phil Zen, feat. Founder Gudni Gudnason

https://www.youtube.com/watch?v=ej9C2_jl-uI

What Did You Learn About Yourself from This Chapter?

[Write about it here]

Epilogue

I have used the story of my life to write this book. But it is just that. A story. It's all true, but it is the barest skeletal outline of my life so far. My purpose for writing this book was about much more. I wanted to inspire you to acknowledge the beauty, goodness, and power that we all hold within us, and to know that you can do anything to which you set your mind. I am reminded how important it is for us to view our lives as a series of stories. They may help us along the way to get from one place to another, but as we move forward, we need to let them go and move on - to our next step, our next stage of life, our next story. Because they really are just stories. And our stories don't matter as much as what we are doing *now* to make a difference in the world.

The more we know ourselves, the more we can serve others. And the more we serve others, the more we come to know ourselves. That's how we change the world. It's really that simple.

I hope I've inspired you to get a life activation and to explore the empowerment that the initiatory path of the Modern Mystery School holds for you. At the very least, I hope I've inspired you to go and find your passion. Our life here on Earth is so short. What makes your heart happy? What feeds your soul? Go. Find that!

I also hope this book has helped you to recognize, to some degree, the stages of Alchemy at work in your life. Just writing this book has been an alchemical process for me. Find the Alchemy in *your* life. The power of Alchemy can be explored in great depth, but ultimately, it's about life! Find the Alchemy in your struggles and in your joys. The magick of Alchemy can be found in every day of our lives. Smile more! Laugh more! Life is Alchemy and Alchemy is life.

Finally, we are not walking this path of life alone. Know that there is a path and a Guide available for all those who seek to understand more, to accelerate their progression, and to serve humanity from a more empowered place. Some of us navigate life better than others, but our navigation will always be better when we have a path to follow and a Guide to guide us. I'd love to help you, in any way I can, to walk a little further in your own progression forward.

Now that I've finished my book, I'm moving on... What's your next step?

About The Author

Dr. Carla Weis received her M.D. from Temple University School of Medicine in Philadelphia, PA. She completed an internship year in Medicine-Pediatrics, completed a residency in Pediatrics at Albert Einstein Medical Center, and a Fellowship in Neonatal-Perinatal Medicine at The Children's Hospital of Philadelphia. She practiced as a hospital-based intensive care physician for nearly 30 years, caring for the smallest of patients, and their families, in NICU's in Pennsylvania, New Jersey, Georgia, Hawaii and California. Since 2011, Dr. Weis has received advanced spiritual training from the Modern Mystery School. She is a certified Healer, Teacher, and Guide in the lineage of King Salomon, as well as an Apprentice of both Alchemy and Universal Hermetic Ray Kabbalah, and owner of Sacred Vibrations, LLC.

Dr. Weis worked as both a hospital clinician and a research scientist, having many academic publications in the field of Pediatrics, Neonatology, and Pulmonology, speaking invitations at many scientific conferences in the United States as well as London, and co-authoring two chapters in a prominent and well-respected Neonatology textbook. On several occasions, she has traveled to Zimbabwe, Africa with Operation of Hope to volunteer her services for mothers and newborns. Dr. Weis was the foreword author for the books, "Ancient Healings, Modern Miracles" and "Holistic Healing Power".

She now focuses her time on assisting and guiding others in their own spiritual progression, creating a sacred and safe space for all. She believes that life is meant to be lived, and that realizing your own true potential is part of thriving as a spiritual and physical being. She has five daughters and four grandchildren, and lives in Huntington Beach, CA.

Contact Information

I live in Huntington Beach, CA. If you live in Southern California, or are visiting, and you would like to work with me, here's what I can offer you:

*Life Activation

*Empower Thyself initiation program

*Many other classes and healings of the King Salomon lineage

Please contact me at:

Email:
Sacredvibrations33@gmail.com

Web site:
www.sacred-vibrations.com

"I am dedicated to your spiritual progression and guiding you along the journey to fulfillment of your life's purpose. Through the enlightenment of you as an individual, I strive to create a wave of change for the betterment of humanity and all beings on the planet." -Carla Weis, MD

Modern Mystery School

If you'd like to explore this Mystery School path for yourself, you don't have to come out to Huntington Beach (although I'd love to have you!). You can simply look on the **modern mystery school** website to "Find a Guide" (via "Connect") in many locations throughout the United States and around the world. If you need help, simply send them an email. (The administrative staff work incredibly hard to answer emails, and they're incredibly nice too! They can help you find whatever you need.)

Website:

www.modernmysteryschoolint.com

Email:

info@modernmysteryschoolint.com

Charitable Donations

A portion of the proceeds from this book will be donated to:

Second Harvest Food Bank

Operation of Hope

Second Harvest Food Bank of Orange County holds the vision of food and nutritional security for all in Orange County, California. Their mission is to provide dignified, equitable and consistent access to nutritious food, creating a foundation for community health.

Operation of Hope is a not-for-profit, all volunteer surgical team that provides free, life-changing, surgical reconstructive care, and healthcare to children in under-served countries.

Resources

BOOKS

Dennis William Hauck, "The Emerald Tablet: Alchemy for Personal Transformation", 1999.

Theresa Bullard, Ph.D., "The Game Changers: Social Alchemists in the 21st Century", 2nd edition, 2021.

Dave Lanyon, "You Are Not Perfect The Way You Are. 11 Keys to Master your Life", 2022.

Dawn Ressel, "Ancient Healings, Modern Miracles. How 3,000-Year-Old Methods are Transforming the Lives of Ordinary People in the 21st Century", 2022.

Ralph H. Blum, "The Book of Runes", 4th edition, 1993.

LINKS

https://www.sacred-vibrations.com/single-post/2018/06/25/what-does-bodybuilding-have-to-do-with-spirituality

https://www.modernmysteryschoolint.com/core-values-and-beliefs/

Printed in the United States
by Baker & Taylor Publisher Services